21世纪英语专业系列教材

向明友
贾　勉
卜晓晖　◇著

语用学导论

PRAGMATICS FOR BEGINNERS

北京大学出版社
PEKING UNIVERSITY PRESS

图书在版编目 (CIP) 数据

语用学导论 / 向明友，贾勉，卜晓晖著 . —北京：北京大学出版社，2022.8
21 世纪英语专业系列教材
ISBN 978-7-301-32935-1

Ⅰ.①语… Ⅱ.①向… ②贾… ③卜… Ⅲ.①英语–语用学–高等学校–教材
Ⅳ.① H313

中国版本图书馆 CIP 数据核字 (2022) 第 105738 号

书　　　名	语用学导论 YUYONGXUE DAOLUN
著作责任者	向明友　贾　勉　卜晓晖　著
责任编辑	刘文静
标准书号	ISBN 978-7-301-32935-1
出版发行	北京大学出版社
地　　　址	北京市海淀区成府路 205 号　100871
网　　　址	http://www.pup.cn　　新浪微博：@ 北京大学出版社
电子邮箱	编辑部 pupwaiwen@pup.cn　　总编室 zpup@pup.cn
电　　　话	邮购部 010-62752015　发行部 010-62750672　编辑部 010-62754382
印　刷　者	北京虎彩文化传播有限公司
经　销　者	新华书店
	720 毫米 ×1020 毫米　16 开本　11.25 印张　377 千字 2022 年 8 月第 1 版　2024 年 11 月第 2 次印刷
定　　　价	52.00 元

未经许可，不得以任何方式复制或抄袭本书之部分或全部内容。
版权所有，侵权必究
举报电话：010-62752024　电子邮箱：fd@pup.cn
图书如有印装质量问题，请与出版部联系，电话：010-62756370

对外经济贸易大学中央高校基本科研业务费
专项资金资助(批准号:18CB03)

Preface by the Professor

Pragmatics for Beginners is the first publication of an introductory series of linguistic studies. While addressing the current call for more introductory and interesting texts in pragmatics, this project aims at developing a new pedagogical practice of preparing undergraduates for advanced studies by compiling introductory textbooks.

Since 2010, I started to teach junior English majors *Introduction to Pragmatics* and wanted to design new assessments to replace the traditional end-of-the-semester exam. In my class, students could receive weighted grades from completing a closed-book exam, writing a course paper, or compiling a textbook. Since textbook compilation is the most difficult option, only two out of 18 students in one class chose this assignment. The present textbook is a revised version of their early efforts, and these two students also become its two co-authors.

I take this project as a systematic training for a global view, critical thinking, and a habit of meticulous observation. Compiling a textbook in its entirety requires students to not only understand individual theories in their local contexts but also sort out the connections among them. Moreover, instead of passively receiving different schools of thought, students will be actively selecting the necessary materials from a larger pool of sources, becoming more cognizant of the pros and cons of different theories. During this assortment, they could become more critical of different theories, generating their critiques of the established paradigms, and developing their perspectives. Finally, to clearly explain the abstract theoretical concepts, students will be motivated to identify interesting and updated instances from their daily communication. Gradually, they are very likely to develop a habit of spotting research questions through their daily experiences. The lively examples they discovered, in turn, could be better received by the beginners who share similar tastes and backgrounds with our student authors. The global awareness enables students to map out the current research trends, the critical awareness enables them to identify niches from the existing scholarships, and the observational awareness enables them to unearth research questions from everyday interactions, reaching both theoretical and social significances. All of these are necessary for the cultivation of a competent researcher.

The present book is the first trial of this pedagogical design. The two student authors have been successfully admitted to renowned graduate programs, one in a Ph. D. program at The University of Texas at Austin, the other in a Master's program at Peking University. Now, I am happy to report this practice to the public, and I hope it can benefit and inspire more young scholars to engage in our research community.

Xiang Mingyou
Oct. 10, 2019

Preface by the Students

This little book is designed by students of pragmatics and aims for younger students of this thriving discipline. Its earliest draft was a course assignment in our junior year to address Professor Xiang's call for interpretations of pragmatics from the learners' perspective. Therefore, we attempt to elaborate on the most basic concepts in pragmatics with up-to-date examples from our students' lives. We hope to offer student readers a fresh perspective to look at pragmatics from the eyes of their peers, to relieve their pain when engaged in academia and to equip them with the upper hand to deal with real-world dilemmas.

The book intends to introduce pragmatics to beginners from three parts: essential topics, research methods, and useful resources. The essential topics follow the British and American traditions, discussing deixis, presupposition, implicature, speech acts, and (im)politeness. Each chapter is developed with both classical examples and down-to-earth illustrations and applications. The final chapter introduces some of the most basic methods and techniques, those have helped us begin our academic journey, to prepare beginners for their own research. The appendixes attach some useful materials as signposts to inspire students to brainstorm beyond this little book and to engage in a larger research community. We hope our work could both contextualize the art of pragmatics in our daily lives and inspire more researchers to elate our living world to academia.

The completion of this textbook is also accredited by a number of rigorous reviewers. We are fully aware of the harms of misunderstandings and misinterpretations that would do to the beginners and the necessity to revise and proofread. Thus, in addition to Professor Xiang's constant guidance and supervision, we have invited professors and Ph. D. students to help us right the ship at various stages of our compilation. They are Dr. Li Xiaochen, Dr. Yang Guoping, Dr. Cao Duxin, Dr. An Yi, Dr. Zhao Yi, Guan Bangdi, Yu Jinghua, Luan Ruiqi, and Zhao Bo. We are also grateful to our peers who offer us lively examples and their own views on pragmatics. They are Yan Caiping, Wang Tong, Zeng Yuan, Shan Ke, Tao Ziyang, Wang Ziyi, and Yang Zhou. Finally, all the mistakes are of course ours.

Jia Mian & Bu Xiaohui
June 28, 2019

CONTENTS

Chapter 1　Introduction ······ (1)
1.1　Definitions of pragmatics ······ (1)
1.2　Meaning and context ······ (2)
1.3　Development of pragmatics ······ (3)
1.4　Organization of the book ······ (6)
1.5　Review ······ (6)

Chapter 2　Deixis ······ (7)
2.1　Preliminaries ······ (7)
2.2　Deictic and non-deictic uses ······ (10)
2.3　Types of deixis ······ (12)
　　2.3.1　Person deixis ······ (12)
　　2.3.2　Time deixis ······ (15)
　　2.3.3　Place deixis ······ (17)
　　2.3.4　Social deixis ······ (18)
　　2.3.5　Discourse deixis ······ (20)
2.4　Applications: Chinese vocatives as pragmatic markers ······ (21)
　　2.4.1　Introduction ······ (21)
　　2.4.2　Vocatives and coherence ······ (22)
　　2.4.3　Vocatives and involvement ······ (24)
　　2.4.4　Vocatives and (im)politeness ······ (25)
2.5　Review ······ (27)

Chapter 3　Presupposition ······ (28)
3.1　Entailment ······ (28)
　　3.1.1　Preliminaries ······ (28)
　　3.1.2　Types of entailment ······ (30)
3.2　Presupposition ······ (31)
　　3.2.1　Preliminaries ······ (31)
　　3.2.2　Types of presupposition ······ (32)
　　3.2.3　Properties of presupposition ······ (34)
　　3.2.4　Presupposition trigger ······ (38)

- 3.3 A comparison between entailment and presupposition ……………………………………… (40)
- 3.4 Applications: Entailment and presupposition in real life ……………………………………………… (41)
  - 3.4.1 English writing ………………………………… (41)
  - 3.4.2 Interpersonal communication ……………… (43)
- 3.5 Review ………………………………………………… (44)

Chapter 4 Implicature ……………………………………… (46)
- 4.1 Preliminaries ………………………………………… (46)
  - 4.1.1 Natural and non-natural meaning ………… (46)
  - 4.1.2 Implicature and implication ………………… (47)
- 4.2 Types of implicature ………………………………… (48)
  - 4.2.1 Conversational and conventional implicatures …………………………………… (48)
  - 4.2.2 Generalized and particularized conversational implicatures …………………………………… (49)
  - 4.2.3 Scalar, alternate, and clausal implicatures …………………………………………………… (50)
- 4.3 Classical Gricean Theory …………………………… (52)
  - 4.3.1 Cooperative principle ………………………… (52)
  - 4.3.2 Creation of conversational implicature …… (53)
  - 4.3.3 Criticisms of Gricean theory ………………… (57)
- 4.4 Neo-Gricean and Post-Gricean Theories ………… (60)
  - 4.4.1 Levinson's Q-, I-, and M-Principles ……… (60)
  - 4.4.2 Horn's Q- and R-Principles ………………… (61)
  - 4.4.3 Sperber & Wilson's Principle of Relevance …………………………………………………… (61)
  - 4.4.4 Retrospections ………………………………… (62)
- 4.5 Properties of conversational implicature ………… (63)
- 4.6 Applications: Exploiting the four Maxims in *Friends* ……………………………………………… (66)
  - 4.6.1 Exploiting the Maxim of Quantity ………… (67)
  - 4.6.2 Exploiting the Maxim of Quality …………… (68)
  - 4.6.3 Exploiting the Maxim of Relation ………… (69)
  - 4.6.4 Exploiting the Maxim of Manner ………… (70)
- 4.7 Review ………………………………………………… (71)

Chapter 5　Speech Acts ……………………………………… (73)
　5.1　Preliminaries ……………………………………… (73)
　　　5.1.1　Performative-constative dichotomy ……… (74)
　　　5.1.2　The performative hypothesis …………… (75)
　5.2　Austin's theorizing of speech acts ………………… (76)
　　　5.2.1　Felicity conditions on performatives ……… (76)
　　　5.2.2　Locutionary, illocutionary, and perlocutionary
　　　　　　 acts ……………………………………… (77)
　　　5.2.3　Types of illocutionary force …………… (78)
　5.3　Searle's theorizing of speech acts ………………… (79)
　　　5.3.1　Felicity conditions on speech acts ………… (79)
　　　5.3.2　Typology of speech acts ……………… (80)
　　　5.3.3　Direct and indirect speech acts ………… (83)
　5.4　Recent developments in Speech Act Theory …… (84)
　　　5.4.1　Study of perlocution ………………… (84)
　　　5.4.2　Classifications of speech acts …………… (86)
　　　5.4.3　Sequencing in speech acts ……………… (88)
　5.5　Speech acts across cultures and contexts ………… (88)
　　　5.5.1　Cross-cultural variations ……………… (88)
　　　5.5.2　Intra-language variations ……………… (89)
　5.6　Applications: Persuasion in Chinese online forum
　　　 requests …………………………………………… (91)
　　　5.6.1　Introduction …………………………… (91)
　　　5.6.2　*Ethos*: Projecting self to the requestees ……… (92)
　　　5.6.3　*Pathos*: Awakening the emotion of the
　　　　　　 requestees ……………………………… (94)
　　　5.6.4　*Logos*: Reasoning with the requestees …… (97)
　5.7　Review …………………………………………… (99)

Chapter 6　Politeness and Impoliteness ……………… (101)
　6.1　Theorizing politeness …………………………… (101)
　　　6.1.1　Characterizing politeness ……………… (102)
　　　6.1.2　Politeness as strategic face management
　　　　　　 …………………………………………… (103)
　　　6.1.3　Politeness as a conversational maxim …… (106)
　　　6.1.4　Politeness as situated evaluation ………… (110)
　6.2　Theorizing impoliteness ………………………… (112)
　　　6.2.1　Types of impoliteness ………………… (112)
　　　6.2.2　Impoliteness as strategic face attacks …… (113)
　　　6.2.3　Impoliteness as conversational maxims … (114)

  6.2.4 Impoliteness as a discursive practice ...... (116)
 6.3 Some potential issues in (im)politeness research .... (116)
 6.4 Applications: Politeness in online forum requests .... (118)
  6.4.1 Introduction .... (118)
  6.4.2 Bald on record strategies .... (119)
  6.4.3 Positive politeness strategies .... (119)
  6.4.4 Negative politeness strategies .... (120)
 6.5 Review .... (121)

Chapter 7 Research Methods .... (123)
 7.1 Literature mining .... (123)
  7.1.1 Four types of exigences .... (123)
  7.1.2 Review articles and bibliographies .... (124)
  7.1.3 Search engines and databases .... (125)
  7.1.4 Bibliometric analysis and knowledge visualization .... (128)
 7.2 Data collection .... (131)
  7.2.1 Interviews .... (131)
  7.2.2 Questionnaires .... (132)
  7.2.3 Discourse completion tests .... (134)
  7.2.4 Role plays .... (134)
  7.2.5 Recordings .... (136)
  7.2.6 Trending methods .... (136)
 7.3 Analytical methods .... (138)
  7.3.1 Conversation analysis and discourse analysis .... (138)
  7.3.2 Statistical analysis .... (146)
 7.4 Review .... (148)

References .... (150)
Appendix One Resources .... (163)
Appendix Two Research Notes .... (166)

Chapter 1

Introduction

In Marvel's film *Thor* (2011), Thor has just been evicted by his father Odin to the human world and is found unconscious by a group of scientists, including Jane, Darcy, and Erik. When Thor wakes up, he tries to find his hammer and wants to return to his home, Asgard. Darcy is shocked by his bluntness and aims at him with a stun gun. After figuring out the hostility of these scientists, Thor is furious and threatens: *You dare threaten me, Thor, with so puny a weapon?* However, before Thor could finish his sentence, Darcy shoots him with her stun gun. The underlying question is why calling out his name carries the power to threaten and why this threat fails to deliver? Language games like this prevail in our daily lives. For example, when your girlfriend asks you about her fitness, why is keeping silent often understood as acquiescence to her being overweight? In fact, people often mean more than what they say. Hence, this book attempts to offer beginners a pragmatic explanation of how people make sense to each other.

The first section discusses the definition of pragmatics; Section 1.2 unpacks some of the important notions in pragmatics; in Section 1.3, the development of pragmatics is recounted; and in the last section, the organization of the entire book is mapped out.

1.1 Definitions of pragmatics

Before discussing the definitions, let's first think about the two underlying questions in the opening scenario: why does Thor think his name could threaten people and why does it fail? First, it is threatening because he is the son of Odin, the god of all gods, and all the people living in the earthly world are under their rule. In other words, by stressing his name, Thor intends to express that he is a powerful person and disobeying him or daring to threaten him will lead to severe punishment. By unpacking Thor's original utterance into its full sense, we could easily understand why it could be threatening. Bearing the answer to the first question in mind, we can also work out why his powerful statement faints. Since Darcy does not know anything about Asgard and Odin, *Thor* means nothing more than a name to her.

However, if it happens in Asgard, no one would dare to shoot Thor with a stun gun since all people know the punitive consequence. In *Avengers: Infinity War* (2018), when Thor shouts out his name, Thanos, the supervillain who knows Thor's identity, still dares to torture him and almost kills him in outer space. This is because Thanos believes that he is much more powerful than Thor and anyone from Asgard and is not afraid of any repercussions of annoying the Asgardians. These two examples show that there are gaps between what the sentence literally means and what the speaker intends to express and how the listener interprets the meaning of the sentence. This special property is called **linguistic underdeterminacy** (Huang, 2014: 8). In other words, the shift of meaning is largely influenced by the change of situations. Bearing these in mind, we shall move to discuss what pragmatics is.

Broadly speaking, **pragmatics** refers to "the study of language use in context" (Huang, 2017: 1). In other words, pragmatics attempts to explain how speakers convey their meaning, and how listeners understand the speaker's meaning. This definition, however, is too vague to account for its complexity. For example, Gazdar (1979) proposes that pragmatics equals meaning without truth condition. Leech (1981) concentrates on how meanings get interpreted in pragmatics. Thomas (1995) entitles her textbook of pragmatics as "meaning in interaction". Yule (1996: 3) straightforwardly states that pragmatics is "the study of speaker meaning". Mey (2001: 6) emphasizes the determinacy of social conditions in pragmatics. Ariel (2010) devotes an entire book to the definition of pragmatics and argues that the distinctive feature of pragmatics is inference based on linguistic outputs. Despite these nuances, all the above definitions seem to emphasize two key notions: meaning and context. In the next section, we will concentrate on these two terms.

1.2 Meaning and context

Our first task is to figure out the meaning of the word *meaning*. In this section, we will distinguish sentence meaning from utterance meaning. Prior to that, we first make a distinction between sentence and utterance. A **sentence** is "a well-formed string of words put together by the grammatical rules of a language" (Huang, 2014: 13), such as *I am Thor*. An **utterance**, however, is the concrete realization of that sentence in a particular situation. To say the above sentence in Asgard or on Earth or to Thanos clearly conveys different meanings and results in distinctive communicative effects.

Sentence meaning, therefore, refers to the abstract meaning of a sentence that is independent of any concrete situations. In Thor's case, the sentence meaning is that the speaker states that his name is Thor. In contrast, **utterance meaning** (speaker meaning) is what the speaker intends to convey via that particular utterance. That is, the utterance meaning of *I am Thor* is to manifest his royal status and ask for utmost respect. To figure out the speaker meaning is the central task of pragmatics.

Furthermore, Leech (1981: 320−321) offers four outward tests for the identification of speaker meaning:

    a. Is reference made to addressers (speakers) or addressees (hearers)?
    b. Is reference made to the intention of the speaker or the interpretation of the hearer?
    c. Is reference made to context?
    d. Is reference made to the kind of act or action performed by means of or by virtue of using language?

The passing of one or more of these four tests is considered as speaker meaning and consequently falls into the discussion of pragmatics.

The second term that needs to be specified is **context**. The traditional understanding of context contains two parts: the linguistic context and the extra-linguistic context. The **linguistic context** refers to the textual environment an utterance is situated in. It could be words, clauses, sentences, paragraphs, or the whole text. In Thor's case, one linguistic context is that the pronoun *I* refers to Thor. In contrast, the **extra-linguistic context** is anything that is nonlinguistic but is relevant to the utterance. It includes but is not limited to temporal (e. g., tomorrow afternoon, in an hour) and spatial information (e. g., in Beijing, next to you) of the utterance, the social status of the speaker, the hearer and anyone referred to in the utterance (e. g., President of the university, my father), and the cultural conventions (e. g., bowing to each other in Japanese culture, accepting compliments in American culture). One important extra-linguistic context is that Thor is the son of Odin, who possesses mighty power. Combining the linguistic and extra-linguistic contexts, hearers can work out that the speaker is making a threat by claiming that he is powerful and should not be offended.

In recent years, more emphases are paid to the dynamic perspective of context. Mey (2001: 39) points out that context is dynamic in that it changes in accordance with the ongoing conversation. This requires scholars to consider the effect of preceding utterances when analyzing a new utterance. This dynamic nature makes Thor's statement effective in one situation and ineffective in another.

1.3 Development of pragmatics

The emergence of pragmatic studies can be traced back to American semiotician and philosopher Charles William Morris in the 1930s. The understanding of pragmatics was mainly formed during his stay at The University of Chicago as an associate professor of philosophy. Partly out of his desire to unify logical positivism with behavioral empiricism and pragmatism, Charles Morris developed a theory of semiotics and offered a trichotomy of syntax, semantics, and pragmatics (Posner, 1987). He notes that **syntax** deals with "the relation of signs to one another"; **semantics** deals with "the relations of signs to the objects to which the signs are applicable"; and **pragmatics** deals with "the signs to interpreters" (Morris, 1938: 6). Following Morris, Carnap (1942) offers a similar trichotomy, in the order of the most concrete to the most abstract, that pragmatics is assigned to where the explicit reference is made to the user of the language, semantics the expressions and what they designate, syntax the relations between the expressions. Morris' and Carnaps' classifications laid the foundation for the development of linguistic studies.

During the 1950s, two loosely constructed philosophical schools of thought, **the school of ideal language philosophy** and **the school of ordinary language philosophy**, largely influenced the development of linguistics. The ideal language philosophers such as Gottlob Frege and Bertrand Russell believe that human language is insufficient to describe the world and hence turn to the quest of the logical system of artificial languages. In contrast, ordinary language philosophers pay more attention to natural language, especially its uses. British philosopher Peter Strawson (1950) challenges Russell's descriptive theory of truth conditions and argues that a sentence can be neither true nor false due to the non-existence of the referent. The clash of ideas between these two schools propels scholars to investigate deixis, how people relate a piece of utterance to a context (Chapter Two) and sentential relationships such as entailment and presupposition (Chapter Three). Moreover, based on the assumption of rationality and mutual cooperation between interlocutors, Paul Grice postulates his theory of Cooperative Principle and conversational implicatures, attempting to explain how people mean more than they say (Chapter Four). In the meantime, John Austin and his student John Searle develop the widely applied theory of Speech Acts to analyze the uses of natural languages, arguing that language is used to do things rather than to simply make statements (Chapter Five). The Cooperative Principle and the Speech Act Theory later become the two backbones of pragmatics.

The above developments, however, primarily reside in the inquiry of language philosophy. The linguistic study of pragmatics is largely advanced by Stephen Levinson. Received a B. A. in Archaeology and Social Anthropology

Chapter 1
Introduction

at Cambridge University and a Ph. D. in Linguistic Anthropology at The University of California, Berkeley, Levinson writes extensively on the matters of pragmatics. His widely celebrated publication *Pragmatics* (1983) is seen as the first comprehensive textbook of this subject that marks the establishment of pragmatics as an independent field①. The matters discussed in this textbook were and remain to be the core issues of today's pragmatic inquiries, such as deixis, presupposition, conversational implicatures, and speech acts.

In addition to these core issues, pragmatics also displays an interdisciplinary nature. Cummings (2005) elaborates in *Pragmatics: A Multidisciplinary Perspective* that pragmatics in its broader sense can be combined with the study of philosophy, psychology, artificial intelligence, and language pathology. Among them, the study of (im)politeness (Chapter Six) appears to be an essential line of research in pragmatics. Furthermore, Horn and Ward (2004: xi) note that

> work in pragmatic theory has extended from the attempt to rescue the syntax and semantics from their own unnecessary complexities to other domains of linguistic inquiry, ranging from historical linguistics to the lexicon, from language acquisition to computational linguistics, from intonational structure to cognitive science.

In short, the studies of pragmatics extend from a "pragmatic wastebasket②" to a multi-disciplinary investigation. On a macro scale, drawing ingredients from sociology, psychology, and computer technology, a large number of sub-disciplines have flourished, including cognitive pragmatics, psycholinguistic pragmatics, computational pragmatics, clinical pragmatics, neuropragmatics, interlanguage pragmatics, sociopragmatics, cultural pragmatics, institutional pragmatics, intercultural pragmatics, variational pragmatics, historical pragmatics, applied pragmatics, corpus pragmatics, literary pragmatics, legal pragmatics, and feminist pragmatics (Huang, 2013). Propelled by the continuous advancement of science and technology, the future of pragmatics could be even more promising.

---

① Verschueren (1999: 2) contends that pragmatics does not constitute a theory of language as syntax and semantics do. Instead, it offers a different **perspective** to language evaluation.

② The term "pragmatic wastebasket" is originated from Israeli philosopher Yehoshua Bar-Hillel's (1971) claim that semantics is a wastebasket of syntax. It refers to a dividing line between semantics and pragmatics that pragmatics is the offcut of truth conditional semantics (Mey, 2001: 19—21).

1.4 Organization of the book

Chapters Two to Six address five classical topics in pragmatics: deixis, presupposition, implicature, speech acts, and (im)politeness. In each topic, we attempt to cover its major concepts as well as some of the heated discussions. After that, we contextualize each of the topics with an empirical study, investigating how pragmatics is reflected in our daily life. At the end of each chapter, readers can find a review that maps out the key notions of that topic. By going through these concepts, learners could self-examine their grasp of each chapter and review accordingly. In Chapter Seven, we introduce some basic research methods for beginners to start their own studies. Finally, in the appendix, we list some useful resources for more detailed research in pragmatics. And now, let's begin our journey from *deixis*.

1.5 Review

- **Linguistic underdeterminacy**
- **Meaning**
    - Sentence and utterance
    - Sentence meaning and utterance meaning
- **Context**
    - Linguistic and extra-linguistic context
    - Dynamic nature
- **History of pragmatics**
    - Trichotomy of syntax, semantics, pragmatics
    - School of ordinary language philosophy
    - School of ideal language philosophy
    - Pragmatic wastebasket
    - Deixis, entailment and presupposition, implicatures, speech acts, (im)politeness, conversation analysis

Chapter 2

Deixis

In Marvel's blockbuster *Black Panther*, King T'Chaka, the sole ruler of Wakanda comes to visit his sister in her laboratory and she shows him two newly designed suits of the Black Panther. When the king utters "this one", we would be puzzled by which suit the king really favors because we have no idea where his finger is pointing at. However, if you have watched this movie, you would know that the king is pointing at a darker suit because it is not too showy. T'Chaka's combination of pointing and uttering "this one" conveys a complete meaning to his sister that he wants to try on the black outfit. This specification of the referent often falls into the use of deixis.

Section 2.1 covers the essential properties of deixis, illustrating its definition, the nature of egocentricity and the deictic projection. In Section 2.2, the distinctions between deictic and non-deictic usages are introduced. Section 2.3 presents five main types of deixis. In the final section, a related case study of Chinese name vocatives is investigated from the perspective of pragmatic markers.

2.1 Preliminaries

The word "deixis" originally means "pointing" via language. It is defined as "the function of grammatical as well as lexical means relating a piece of language to its context in terms of its users, the time and place of its occurrence, and the people and objects it refers to" (Jiang, 2000: 11). That is, deixis is used to ensure that the context is specific enough for the hearer to work out the pragmatic meaning of a given utterance. The common grammatical and lexical means include demonstratives (e.g., *this*, *that*), first- and second-person pronouns (e.g., *I*, *you*), tense markers (e.g., *-ed*, *-ing*), adverbs of time and space (e.g., *now*, *there*), and motion verbs (e.g., *go*, *come*) (Huang, 2014: 169). In the opening example, T'Chaka specifies the demonstrative "this" by pointing at a particular suit he prefers, ensuring that his sister understands his preference. However, since demonstratives include both *this* and *that*, what determines the speaker's choice of a proximal term (this) over a distal term (that)? This concerns the issue of the **deictic center**.

Generally speaking, deixis is self-centered: "(1) the central person is the speaker, (2) the central time is the time at which the speaker produces the utterances, (3) the central place is the speaker's location at utterance time, (4) the discourse center is the point which the speaker is currently at in the production of his utterance, and (5) the social center is the speaker's social status and rank, to which the status or rank of addressees or referents is relative" (Levinson, 1983: 64). This self-centered organization is called the **egocentricity** of deixis. In *Black Panther*, when T'Chaka's long-separated cousin N'Jadaka comes back to Wakanda for revenge, T'Chaka warns him that this is his last chance to surrender. N'Jadaka responds that

(2.1) I lived my entire life waiting for this moment ... just so I could kill you.

Black Panther (2018)

Following the aforementioned self-centeredness, we could infer that the central person *I* refers to N'Jadaka and he wants to kill the king at the present time in the exact place where he stands. If the king retorts:

(2.2) That's not gonna happen, brother.

Then the deictic center automatically shifts to T'Chaka, the addressee in the preceding utterance. The use of *that* instead of *this* shows that the threat was made by the hearer not the speaker and thus is distant from the current discourse center, i.e., T'Chaka's point of view. Finally, following egocentricity, *brother* in 2.2 suggests that the addressee is a brother to the speaker, not to anyone else.

Therefore, it is essential for interlocutors to bear this egocentric use of deixis in mind, especially when they are not in a face-to-face conversation or they are not in the same place or at the same time of speaking. The common media include e-mails, letters, postcards, cellphones, WeChat, WhatsApp, Messenger, Facebook, etc. For example, one needs to realize that "five score years ago" mentioned in Martin Luther King Jr.'s speech is a century earlier than the time he gave the speech in 1963 rather than a century before the year you read this book.

It is also worth noting that egocentricity sometimes can be violated on the following two occasions: First, in some languages, the use of demonstratives is, in part, determined by the addressee. In Japanese, the choice of demonstratives is jointly decided by both the speaker and the hearer. The demonstrative *sore* refers to the place that is close to the hearer and distant from the speaker, whereas *are* is used in cases where the referent is both away from the speaker and the hearer. Second, the speaker purposefully projects himself into a deictic context centered on the addressee, so as to express empathy or politeness. See the following two examples:

(2.3) *Tom is Mary's boyfriend. And Tom just learned that Mary is sick and he wanted to visit. Compare the two messages Tom might send to Mary:*
   a. I will GO to your apartment as soon as possible.
   b. I will COME to your apartment as soon as possible.

In both (2.3a) and (2.3b), Tom conveys a clear message that he will visit Mary very soon. A close comparison between *come* and *go*, however, shows that Tom considers himself as the center in (2.3a), whereas Mary is placed at the deictic center in (2.3b). Compared to (2.3a), (2.3b) not only conveys the message of Tom's quick arrival but also places Mary as his center, revealing his considerateness. Moreover, when arranging appointments in international contexts, it is also customary to specify the scheduled time in accordance with the receiver's time zone: the organizers of a conference often project the central time to the participants by indicating Beijing Time for Chinese and Tokyo Time for Japanese. This deictic projection reduces the chances of miscalculation of appointment, showing the organizers' consideration and ensuring the efficiency of the conference. Deictic projection has recently been made automatic in some online arrangement applications, as shown in the following Doodle interview form sent by a professor from America to students in China:

(2.4) Doodle sheet for graduates' interview of an American university

All times displayed in Asia/Shanghai

Only you and Xiaoli Nan can see your vote and comments.

Table   Calendar

	Jan 13 SAT	Jan 13 SAT	Jan 13 SAT	Jan 13 SAT	Jan 14 SUN
	12:00 PM 12:29 PM	12:30 PM 12:59 PM	10:00 PM 10:29 PM	10:30 PM 10:59 PM	12:00 PM 12:30 PM
? participants					
Enter your name					

In short, the pragmatic use of deixis concerns not only the precision of reference but also the humanistic side of interpersonal communication. In the following section, we will expound the deictic and anaphoric uses of deixis.

2.2 Deictic and non-deictic uses

Deixis can be used both deictically and non-deictically. Deictic expressions refer to the expressions with deictic use as their central usage, whereas the non-deictic expressions have non-deictic use as their major function. For example, the second-person pronoun is a common deictic expression, as shown in (2.5), whereas the third-person pronoun is usually an anaphora and thus a non-deictic use, as shown in (2.6).

(2.5) *You* and *you*, stand up!
(2.6) John believes that *he* will definitely win the prize.

When deixis is used to link a piece of language and its context, we call these words **deictics**. And they are also frequently referred to as indexical expressions or indexicals in the literature of philosophy (Huang, 2014: 169). Deictics can be subdivided into gestural and symbolic uses. The use of deictic expressions together with paralinguistic features is called the **gestural use**, and that without the **symbolic use**. Paralinguistic features include eye-gaze, facial expressions, nodding, hand gestures, and unusual variations of pitch, loudness, and duration of sound. The proximal deictics like *this*, *now*, and *here* refer to things nearby, usually in a gestural way. The distal deictics, those for distant reference, are more often used in a symbolic manner. See the examples below:

(2.7) *This* one is genuine, but *this* one is fake.
(2.8) *You*, *you*, but not *you* are dismissed.
(2.9) What did *you* say?
(2.10) I'm working on a new book *now*.
(2.11) *This* city is really beautiful.

Examples (2.7) and (2.8) are gestural in nature. Without pointing at a particular referent, the hearer would be hard to know which item is fake in (2.7) and which persons are dismissed in (2.8). Case (2.9), however, can be seen as either symbolic or gestural. For instance, when a professor is talking to a student in front of the class, he is more likely to specify the addressee by pointing to a particular student and thus gestural. In contrast, when it comes to a private appointment, both interlocutors have very clear understandings of the addressee, and thus it is used symbolically. In (2.10), without any assistance of paralanguage, the hearer can easily work out the meaning of "now". The final example often falls into the category of symbolic use. One, however, may contend that it is also a gestural use because we could point at a city on the map. Even though we could take out a map and gesture the city, it

Chapter 2
Deixis

is still not the real referent and hence belongs to the symbolic use.

Non-deictic use involves both anaphoric and non-anaphoric uses (Levinson, 1983: 67). The key difference is that anaphoric use requires co-reference with its antecedent in the same sentence or discourse. In the meantime, the antecedent must have a higher position in the constituent structure of the sentence than the pronoun. See the following examples:

(2.12) My friend looked up when *he* came in.
(2.13) When *he* came in, my friend looked up.
(2.14) My friend looked up when *HE* came in. (unusual stress)
(2.15) *He* came in and my friend looked up.

In both (2.12) and (2.13), *he* is co-referent with the antecedent *my friend*. In (2.12), the pronoun *he* is used in a typical anaphoric sense. When the pronoun precedes the antecedent, as shown in (2.13), this co-reference is called **cataphora**. In contrast, (2.14) is not an anaphoric use because the unusual stress indicates that it is a different person compared with "my friend". And the pronoun *he* in (2.15) is also used non-anaphorically in that it is not governed by the antecedent *my friend*, viz. they are placed on the same syntactic level in this case.

Finally, it is worth noting that deictic expressions can also be used in a non-deictic sense, as in (2.16), and a non-deictic expression can function in a deictic way, as in (2.17) (Huang, 2014: 171). Moreover, a deictic term can also be used both anaphorically and deictically, as in (2.18) (Lyons, 1977b: 676, see also Levinson, 1983: 67).

(2.16) If *you* escape the movie ticket, *you* will be fined heavily.
(2.17) *She*'s not the actress; *she* is. *She*'s the understudy.
(2.18) I was born in Beijing and have lived *there* ever since.

In a nutshell, the uses of deixis could be classified into deictic and non-deictic uses. The deictic use can be further divided into gestural and symbolic uses, while non-deictic use involves both anaphoric and non-anaphoric uses. The gestural use could only be accurately understood with the assistance of perceptibly physical elements of the speech act[①], whereas the symbolic use requires the perception of certain aspects of the communicative situation. This

---

[①] The gestural use of deictics can also be assisted by the direction of sound. For instance, before getting off the train, the train attendant often says that "please get off from the door on this side of the coach". Even if the hearer does not see where the attendant is or where he is pointing at, the passenger can still understand what "this" refers to as long as he is able to tell where the attendant's sound comes from.

is summarized as follows:

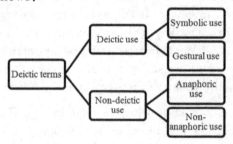

2.3 Types of deixis

This section illustrates the five main types of deictics corresponding to the five parameters of egocentricity proposed by Levinson in Section 2.1, i.e., person, time, space, social, and discourse. The first three types are the most commonly used deictic terms and they are often used with paralinguistic assistance (Mey, 2001: 54), whereas the last two types are associated with contextual features.

2.3.1 Person deixis

Person deixis contributes to the identification of the interlocutors or participant-roles in a speech event (Huang, 2014: 174). The two common types of person deixis are **personal pronouns** and **vocatives**. The former involves the use of different pronouns and their syntactic agreements, while the latter consists of proper names, kinship terms, titles, and general terms, etc.

Personal pronouns involve a three-way distinction of first, second, and third persons. The most fundamental mode of communication is between "I" and "You". The use of pronouns usually conveys the number and the gender of the interlocutors. Let's start with participant-roles.

In a speech event, both interlocutors are potential addressers and addressees. However, there could be only one speaker/addresser at the production of an utterance, whereas multiple hearers/listeners may be involved in one utterance. Although only one person can speak at a given point, he or she often uses the plural form "we" when representing a group of people. When releasing a new version of the iPhone, Mr. Tim Cook would wisely choose to use "we" to indicate the joint contribution made by the entire research and development team. Hearers/listeners can be divided into addressee and bystander. At Apple's annual conference, all the reporters, Apple fans and anyone interested in their products belong to the addressees that the company wants to impress. Although those security guards at the venue are also able to hear the promotion, they generally are not who the company intends to impress and therefore are considered as bystanders. In a conversation, the former is represented by second-person pronouns, and the latter is addressed via third-person pronouns. The relationship between different types of pronouns is summarized as follows:

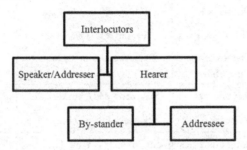

Pronouns also distinguish number and gender in different languages. The singular and plural of second-person pronoun are both expressed via "you" in English but via *ni* (singular) and *nimen* (plural) separately in Chinese. Moreover, there is a distinction between exclusive "we" (excluding addressee) and inclusive "we" (including both speaker and addressee) in English (Yule 1996: 11). See the examples (2.19—2.20) below:

(2.19) Let us go to see a movie. (exclusive we)
(2.20) Let's go to see a movie. (inclusive we)

There are also gender differences among different languages. In all languages with pronominal gender marking, gender differences can be found on third persons (e.g., English, Russian, Catalan, Marathi) (Huang, 2014: 178); some languages can be marked on both second- and third-person pronouns, such as traditional Chinese and Modern Hebrew (Anderson & Keenan, 1985: 269); finally, in Nagla, one can tell gender from first person (Trudgill, 2000: 63). Moreover, some languages only mark the singular form and some others only mark a particular gender. For instance, English pronouns mark the third-person singular (*he* or *she*), while the third person plural is unmarked (using *they* for both genders). In modern Chinese, third-person plural only marks the female group, and interlocutors cannot identify if it is a group with all males or with both males and females.

In addition to personal pronouns, vocatives also function as name deixis. In general, vocatives are defined as "noun phrases that refer to the addressee but are not syntactically or semantically incorporated as the arguments of a predicate" (Levinson, 1983: 71). A brief typology of vocatives is presented below in (2.21) (see Leech, 1999 for detailed studies in English and Xiang, 1995 in Chinese).

(2.21) A brief typology of Chinese and English vocatives

Types	Sub-types	English	Chinese
Names	Full name	Tom Cruise, Meghan Markle	吴京,钱锺书,闫彩萍
	First name	Thor, Steve, Donald	子怡,笃鑫,国萍
	Last name	Trump, Markle, Jobs	南宫,慕容,长孙
	Names with modifiers	Thor the god of thunder, Jack the ripper	小张,阿宏,老李头,强子,童童
Kinship terms	Direct addressing	Sis, bro, dad, auntie, kid	老爸,王叔,婶儿
	Indirect addressing	Son of Odin (Odinson)	孩子他爸,她哥
Occupational titles	Prestigious titles	Your Majesty, Your Highness	王主席,李处
	Common titles	Solider, officer, Doctor Strange	张教授,王秘书
Evaluative terms	Positive evaluations	Pretty, genius	李老,大虾(大侠),大师
	Negative evaluations	Asshole, you idiot	瘸子,你个笨蛋,挨千刀的
	Neutral evaluations	Ma'am, Sir, man, guys, y'all, dude	先生,师傅,同志,同学,帅哥,美女

Here are three caveats of using vocatives. First, in Chinese, only dissyllabic last names can be used as vocatives without other modifiers, whereas monosyllabic last names have to be bound with other modifiers (e. g., *Laozhang*, *Zhanglaoshi*, *Wangshu*). Chao (1965/2011: 527) noted that "the force of compounding between a monosyllabic surname and a monosyllabic given name is so strong that even a wife sometimes calls a husband, less frequently a husband calls a wife, by his (or her) full name." In contrast, English last names are free. Last names without any modifiers are often used in institutionalized contexts such as courts and parliaments.

Second, Chinese kinship terms can be uttered to both family members (kin use) and people without blood ties (non-kin use). The non-kin use usually shares the properties of conventionality and detachability. On the one hand, non-kin uses are highly conventionalized, so that only certain words can be used as vocatives, e. g., *yeye* (grandfather, used for addressing people as old as the speaker's grandfather), *shushu* (uncle, used for addressing people as old as the speaker's father or slightly younger, *gege* (elder brother, used for addressing people only several years older than the speaker). Others kinship terms such as *laoye* (grandfather from mother's side), *baba* (father) cannot address non-family members. On the other hand, non-kin uses can be bound with both surnames and given names, while kin uses can only be connected with given names. For example, Jack Ma, the founder of Alipay, is frequently referred to as *Ma baba* for acknowledging his business success rather than indicating a blood relation.

Third, evaluative terms are dynamic in accordance with socio-cultural factors and contextual factors. In other words, a positive evaluation term could convey a negative meaning when used ironically, whereas a negative term could also boost interpersonal relationship, examples of which could often be seen among Chinese couples or very close friends and relatives, such as *nigelaobuside* (you who are too old to live), *aiqiandaode* (the one who deserves death by a thousand cuts), *xiaoshagua* (little idiot), *zhunaodai* (pig head).

This section mainly discusses vocatives from the perspective of participant-roles. The function of social indexing will be elaborated in Section 2.3.4 and a case study of its pragmatic functions will be presented in Section 2.4.

2.3.2 Time deixis

Time deixis, or temporal deixis, measures the encoding of temporal points and spans coordinating to the time at which an utterance was produced. The two main types of time deixis are time adverbials (e.g., *yesterday*, *tomorrow*, *now*, *then*, etc.) and tense (e.g., *-ed*, *-ing*, etc.)

Our discussion starts with time adverbials. In general, time can be represented through calendrical and non-calendrical ways. The **calendrical time** measures a fixed period of naturally given temporal unit, such as *3 o'clock*, *Monday*, and *November 19*, *1993*. In contrast, **non-calendrical** use refers to the time measurements that are relative to some definite time units, such as *yesterday*, *today*, *tomorrow*, and *two days ago*. The calendrical and non-calendrical uses are shown in (2.22) and (2.23) respectively.

(2.22) Please hand in your homework on November 19, 2017.
(2.23) Please hand in your homework tomorrow.

A sophist, however, may take advantage of the non-calendrical coding by subsequently changing the referred time in relation to "tomorrow". He might argue with the teacher by saying that "you said we need to hand in homework tomorrow, but now in today, not tomorrow". The next day, he can play the same trick when the teacher asks him for homework. What this sophist student was trying to mix up is the coding time and the receiving time of an utterance. The **coding time** is the time at which the speaker produces the utterance, and the **receiving time** refers to the time at which the hearer receives the utterance. In face-to-face communications, the coding time coincides with the receiving time and consequently, the speaker and the hearer share the same coordinate in the non-calendrical span. In non-face-to-face communications, such as WeChat message or voicemail recording; however, the speaker needs to decide whether or not to keep the deictic center on himself or to project it onto the hearer. Conversely, the hearer is also responsible to discern the coding time from the receiving time.

An interesting point is that the non-calendrical terms often carry a preemptive nature of usage compared to calendrical terms. As shown in (2.22) and (2.23), if "tomorrow" were "November 19, 2017", the speaker would be inclined to use the non-calendrical term. This preemptive nature commonly exists in synchronic communications, whereas it could be violated in asynchronous communication where the coding time is not identical to its receiving time. For example, if the course instructor wants to post his assignment deadline on the Internet, it would be clearer to choose (2.22) over (2.23). In fact, people could be very likely to mix up time in midnight. The writer thought that it was still the late evening on November 19; however, the earth rotation has carried him to the early morning of November 20. A careless teacher will be surprised to find that all his students will not submit their homework until the 20th if he chooses to write "tomorrow" and post the notice at midnight.

The switch between calendrical and non-calendrical uses is also determined by the lexical richness of a language. For example, English only has one lexicalized deictic term to describe one day before and after the coding time, i.e., yesterday and tomorrow. Chinese, however, can describe two days before and after the coding time, i.e., *qiantian* "the day before yesterday", *zuotian* "yesterday", *mingtian* "tomorrow", and *houtian* "the day after tomorrow" respectively (arguably the third pair *daqiantian* "three days ago" and *dahoutian* "three days later").

The second type of time deixis is tense. One needs to distinguish between **metalinguistic tense** (M-tense) and **linguistic tense** (L-tense) (Lyons, 1977: 682; Levinson, 1983: 77). M-tense refers to the theoretical category of tense, including the past tense and the present tense. L-tense is the linguistic realization of M-tense in different forms. For example, the difference between the present continuous tense and the present perfect tense is not on the M-tense but the L-tense level. In a strict sense, they are two different aspects of the present tense, i.e., how the speaker chooses to describe the action: the present continuous tense indicates that the speaker intends to describe the present action as ongoing and has not been finished yet; the present perfect tense suggests that the speaker thinks that the action is complete and projects certain influence on the present time. It is worth noting that every language has M-tense but not all languages are marked with L-tense. For instance, Chinese has no markings on the verb in different time spans, but the tense can be worked out through sentence meaning, as shown in (2.24).

(2.24) a. 他喜欢吃庆丰包子。(simple present tense)
b. 他计划明天吃庆丰包子。(simple future tense)
c. 他正在吃庆丰包子。(present continuous tense)

Tense can be used to locate the time of the speech event in relation to the coding time or to identify its distance from reality. The present tense is the proximal form and the past tense is the distal form. See the examples below:

(2.25) I live in Beijing.
(2.26) I lived in New York.
(2.27) Beijing is the capital city of China.
(2.28) If I were you, I would love to go to Beijing.

In (2.25), without time adverbials, one can still infer that the speaker is living in Beijing now at the production time of the utterance. In contrast, the use of past tense in (2.26) suggests that the speaker used to live in New York and no longer live there at the coding time. The present tense in (2.27) shows that the utterance is a statement of truth, whereas the subjunctive mood in (2.28) distances the utterance from the reality because the addresser "I" can never become the addressee "you". When used in suggestions, the subjunctive mood could convey a degree of politeness because it indicates that what the speaker suggested is not necessarily imperative but optional, leaving the addressee a space to decide by herself.

2.3.3 Place deixis

Place deixis, or space deixis, spatial deixis, concerns the specification of locations relative to the reference point at the production time of the utterance. Similar to time deixis, place deixis is also constructed by the interaction of deictic coordinates with the non-deictic perception (Levinson, 1983: 73). While it is possible for the addresser and the addressee to share at the same time, it is impossible for them to occupy the same location. The common space deixes are demonstratives (e.g., *this*, *that*), deictic adverbs of space (e.g., *here*), and deictic directionals (e.g., *come*, *go*).

Place deixis can be used to suggest both physical and psychological distances. See the following examples.

(2.29) *That* woman is a politician and *this* one is only a waitress.
(2.30) *At the White House press conference held on the 21 January 1998 when Bill Clinton made a statement about his relationship with Miss Lewinsky.*

Clinton: I did not have sexual relations with *that* woman. (Huang 2014: 219)

In (2.29), *that* is used as a distal form of deixis to refer to the female politician who stands away in comparison to the waitress "close" in terms of physical location. In (2.30), however, choosing *that* does not necessarily mean that Miss Lewinsky was standing far away from President Clinton at the coding time of that statement (In fact, she was not present in that press conference at all). What President Clinton was more likely to convey is the message that he was psychologically distant from Miss Lewinsky in the sense that they were only coworkers but not sexual partners. This is a deictic use on the psychological level. This special type of place deixis is also called empathic deixis (Levinson, 1983; Lyons, 1977b) or emotional deixis (Huang, 2014).

Another point that needs to be stressed is that place deixis can be encoded based on either the addresser or the addressee's coordinates, generating different inferred meanings. Take the following motion verbs as examples.

(2.31) I will *come* to your office soon.
(2.32) I will *go* to your office soon.

Examples (2.31) and (2.32) can be interpreted in two different ways. Following the egocentric use of deixis, we can infer that the speaker in (2.31) is close to the office, whereas the addressee in (2.32) is close to the office. However, when considered as a deictic projection, the speaker could also be away from the office in (2.31), and the addressee could be standing close to the speaker and being far away from the office.

2.3.4 Social deixis

Social deixis is used to indicate the social status of the involved persons in discourse and marks the social relationship held between them. There are basically two types of socially deictic information: absolute and relational (Levinson, 1983: 90). The former refers to the reserved terms for referent with special social status, e.g., *Her Majesty*, *Your Highness*, *Mr. President* in English and *zhen*, *gu* in Chinese (*Zhen* and *gu* are privileged self-addressing terms for emperors and kings in ancient China).

The relational information in social deixis is more widely used and can be grouped into four categories: speaker and referent (e.g., referent honorifics), speaker and addressee (e.g., addressee honorifics), speaker and bystander (e.g., bystander or audience honorifics), and speaker and setting (e.g., levels of formality) (Levinson, 1983: 90). The difference between **referent honorifics** and **addressee honorifics** is that the former has to show respect by mentioning the referent, whereas the latter can express respect without referring to the target (Comrie, 1976). For example, the distinction between *tu/vous* forms in French is a referent honorific where the referent happens to be the addressee. In contrast, the choice between *yongshan* "to eat (for the royal family)" and *chifan* "to eat (for ordinary citizens)" is a common addressee honorific in Chinese. **Bystander honorifics** are terms that are used to show respect to the bystanders of a speech event, including the audience and the non-participants. Finally, the levels of formality are also in accordance with different social settings. A common example is that one would choose *to dine* in English or *yongcan* in Chinese on a formal occasion while using *to eat* in English or its Chinese counterpart *chifan* in an informal setting.

Following the illustration of person deixis in Section 2.3.1, we expound on the relationship between person deixis and social deixis. In general, social deixis can be seen as an extension of person deixis. Person deixes such as personal pronouns and vocatives are also social deixes. The major difference is that person deixis concerns more about the participant-roles, whereas social deixis focuses on the choice of different honorific forms for a particular person in a specific context. Addressers employ social deixis to convey his or her respect, care, or closeness to the involved participants in a speech event. Alternatively, the choice of such expressions implies the degree of social distance or social closeness between the addresser and other participants. For example, in Chinese, the use of *ni/nin* "you" indicates that the utterance is directed to the addressee, not the bystander, but the choice between *ni* and *nin* suggests the social relationship held between the addresser and the addressee. The use of *ni*, the informal addressing terms, shows a high degree of solidarity or a low degree of power difference. In contrast, using the formal addressing term *nin* reveals a larger power difference between the interlocutors. A similar difference can also be found in the *tu/vous* distinction in French where *tu* represents a close social distance and *vous* denotes a larger power difference (Brown & Gilman, 1960).

More importantly, since most of the social deixes are relational and subject to change, the appropriate manipulation of these deictics could enhance the pragmatic force of a speech act. For instance,

(2.33) *Penny and Leonard are voting yes to remove Sheldon from the Tenants Association. Sheldon is trying to get a no vote from Amy.*

Sheldon: Not so fast. I believe we have one tenant here who has not made her voice heard.
Amy: Oh.
Sheldon: We're waiting, fiancée.
Penny: Yeah, we're waiting, best friend.
Leonard: Yeah, we're waiting, neighbor who needed a battery and totally got one from me, no strings attached.

The Big Bang Theory (2018)

In the above scenario, in order to win Amy's vote, Sheldon manifests his special relationship with Amy by saying *fiancée*. In so doing, Amy is more likely to vote for Sheldon to vindicate her determination to protect her better half, which is generally expected in marriage. Likewise, Penny also manages to display affinity with Amy by stressing that she is her best friend. Finally, despite having no special bond with Amy, Leonard still tries to create a seemingly intimate relation with Amy by reminding her that he used to lend her a battery with no strings attached. The strategic showcasing of social relationship enhances the pragmatic force of the speech act from each speaker and hence puts Amy into a more complicated dilemma.

2.3.5 Discourse deixis

The final category of deixis is **discourse deixis** or textual deixis. It concerns the use of linguistic expressions within some utterances to refer to the current, preceding, or following utterance in the same discourse. Since a discourse consists of complete utterances, there is no denying that sometimes it unfolds time, space and other elements. Hence, both time deixis and space deixis could be employed to anchor some part of the discourse. See the illustrative examples below (deictics are italicized):

(2.34) As mentioned in the *last* chapter, pragmatics can be regarded as a study of meaning.
(2.35) In the *next* section, I will introduce social deixis to the class.
(2.36) I believe that you do not know *this* rumor about Tony.
(2.37) *That* was the happiest moment I have ever enjoyed.

Utterances (2.34) and (2.35) employ time deictic expressions *last* and *next* respectively as the referents to anchor some portion of the preceding and the forthcoming discourse. Examples (2.36) and (2.37) use space deictic expressions *this* and *that* to refer to some part of the **co-text**, the preceding and the following discourse. An interesting point is that if we analyze the deictic expressions with other elements of the utterance, we could find that time deixes *last* and *next* assume a kind of space prominence in the whole context, while space deixes *this* and *that* are situated in a temporal dimension.

Furthermore, utterance initial usages of relative adverbials such as *anyway*, *however*, *but*, *although*, *thus*, *hence*, *so*, *in conclusion*, *well*, *besides*, *all in all*, and *after all* can also signal a cohesive relationship of the utterance in the same discourse. A major function of this use is to link the present utterances with some portions of the preceding utterances (Huang, 2014: 217; Levinson, 1983: 87—88).

A final category of discourse deixis is topic marking in some topic prominent languages (e.g. Chinese and Japanese) (Huang, 2014: 217—218).

For example,

(2.38) 安全问题,我们大家都要重视。

Following the analysis in Li and Thompson (1976), the topic takes precedence over the subject in controlling co-reference. In other words, it is not *women* "us" but *anquan wenti* "the matter of safety" is the given information. Even without given contexts, we could infer that *the matter of safety* must refer to the previous discussion about an incidence of safety. Therefore, we can observe that the topic marking clearly connects the preceding discourse with the current and perhaps the following utterances.

Finally, we draw a distinction between discourse deixis and anaphora. In general, discourse deixis refers to a portion of the discourse, whereas anaphora refers to the same entity expressed earlier (cataphora refers to the same entity which is identified later or subsequently). Here are several examples:

(2.39) a. James exerted all his energy into a new career, and in the end, *he* became a successful businessman.
b. Once *she* finished the course paper, Xiaohui flew to Hong Kong for a summer school.

(2.40) Dr. Xiang introduced the five types of deixis and then Xiaohui did *it* to James.

In (2.39), the pronoun *he* is used anaphorically and co-referential with the antecedent *James* while *she* is used cataphorically and co-referential with the postcedent *Xiaohui*. Since the two pronouns refer to the same referent in each discourse, they are not deixis. On the other hand, in (2.40), the pronoun *it* does not refer to what has appeared before but represents the task of retelling the types of deixis to James. In this case, the pronoun *it* is used deictically.

2.4 Applications: Chinese vocatives as pragmatic markers

As we can see from the introduction of five major types of deixis, the uses of personal pronouns and vocatives occupy a huge chunk of deictic usage, i.e., person deixis and social deixis. As a classic topic in pragmatics, the study of pragmatic markers holds a strong tie with the study of vocatives (Fraser, 1996, 2006). In this section, we attempt to illustrate the use of Chinese name vocatives as pragmatic markers. Section 2.4.1 introduces the research design of the case study and the following three sections present the realizations of the three main functions of pragmatic markers in Chinese vocatives.

2.4.1 Introduction

This study adopts Fraser's (1996) classification of vocatives as pragmatic markers and Aijmer's (2015: 201) tripartite of their pragmatic functions. Pragmatic markers are commonly understood as a group of words that do not constitute the propositional content but contain pragmatic functions in speech. Vocatives are defined as "noun phrases that refer to the addressee but are not syntactically or semantically incorporated as the arguments of a predicate" (Levinson, 1983: 71). Therefore, vocatives can be analyzed in the framework of pragmatic markers.

The data are extracted from the TV program subcategory of CCL (Center for Chinese Linguistics) Corpus. TV programs are largely constituted of spoken language and can best reflect the use of vocatives in conversations. This sub-corpus consists of 44 texts, containing 4 million characters (4,374,300). Since vocatives are usually separated by a comma in transcripts, in CCL corpus, we use regular expressions ",＄5。" "。＄5," ",＄5," respectively to extract phrases with no more than five words between two punctuations. We extracted 390 vocatives from our corpus. The following three sections introduce their pragmatic functions of coherence, involvement, and (im)politeness.

2.4.2 Vocatives and coherence

Vocatives carry the property of coherence. They are "the grease between the propositional parts of discourse making it work as discourse and they can create coherence 'locally' within the speaker's turn" (Aijmer, 2013: 32). This textual function is achieved with strong connections to the positioning of vocatives. We identify five sub-functions under this category: turn-initiating, turn-maintaining, turn-taking, turn-offering, and topic-shifting.

Vocatives are frequently used in getting the addressee's attention and therefore initiating a conversation. This function is achieved in utterance initial, as shown in (2.41).

(2.41) *Lin Xiaofeng is mad at her husband Song Jianping for his extramarital affairs. She doesn't want to go to a party together with Song and is leaving*:
宋建平：小枫，走，洗把脸，去！跟我一块儿去！

《中国式离婚》(2004)

Since Lin Xiaofeng has gone far, by shouting out her name, Song Jianping is trying to get her attention so as to invite her again to join the party.

Similarly, name vocatives can be used to maintain the ongoing conversation. By calling the addressee's name, the speaker conveys his willingness to hold his position to speak.

(2.42) *Liang Bida and Chen Mohan are having a long conversation at*

Chapter 2
Deixis

night.
梁必达:现在,该是我们两个蓝桥埠娃子谈点私事的时候了。墨涵,还记得韩秋云吗?

《历史的天空》(2004)

In (2.42), Liang Bida has finished discussing business with Chen Mohan and wants to talk about something private. By uttering Mohan's name, Liang not only maintains his position to continue speaking but further explains the details of "something private", connecting these two pieces of utterances.

Conversely, name vocatives can also be used to take turns in the struggle of conversing. For instance,

(2.43) *Xiao Li is trying to flirt with Song Jianping*:
肖莉: 老宋,你在新单位里是不是有一种如鱼得水的感觉?
宋建平:如鱼得水谈不上,比较适合我而已。外企的人事关系相对要简单,我这人就简单。
肖莉: 是,简单。单纯,善良,可爱……
宋建平:打住,肖莉,打住。不要再挑逗我,不要再给我错觉,不要再让我瞧不起你……

《中国式离婚》(2004)

In the above scenario, Song Jianping has had enough of Xiao's flirting and therefore interrupts her when she is listing Song's good qualities. By uttering Xiao's full name, Song obstructs Xiao's flow, seizing an opportunity to decline her affection.

Instead of struggling to take the position to speak, interlocutors can also use vocatives to invite bystanders, particularly the ones the current speaker intends to address, to participate in the ongoing discourse. For instance,

(2.44) *Ge Ling, Yu Deli, and Li Dongbao are discussing a solution to remedy a mistake they made earlier*:
戈玲: 我们年轻人也不会让你们顶这雷。是不是,东宝,得利?
余得利:没错儿。
戈玲: 我们惹出的麻烦,我们绝不会推诿。
李东宝:对。

《编辑部的故事》(1991)

(2.45) *Zhang Pujing, Liang Bida, Dou Yuquan, and Zhu Yudao are planning for a critical rescue of their comrade from the enemy*.
张普景:炮不比枪,恐怕没那么精确的。老梁,这个决心还得你下。
梁必达:不能打,炮手卸弹。(对朱预道)你是什么意思,想杀人灭口吗?……

《历史的天空》(2004)

In (2.44), by articulating Dongbao and Deli's names, Ge Ling offers the chance to speak to the two hearers, attempting to seek their agreement on reassuring their willingness to shoulder the responsibility. In (2.45), facing the potential collateral damage to their comrades, Zhang Pujing hands the decision power to the commander Liang Bida by addressing him among the members of the leadership. In both cases, the designated hearers respond immediately, fulfilling the pragmatic function of turn-offering.

Finally, with regard to discourse management, name vocatives are effective in finishing the current topic and initiating a new topic.

(2.46) *Xiaochu and Captain Xie are investigating a murder case*:
小楚:似乎案犯只想偷一点儿钱,但被死者发现了。谢队,这个案子是上报支队还是由我们分队刑警大队处理?

《冬至》(2003)

In (2.46), the speaker is briefing Captain Xie about the whole story between the criminal and the victim. The occupational vocative *xiedui* wraps up the first part of the discourse and shifts to the second topic, asking if they should handle this case by themselves or report to their supervisors.

2.4.3 Vocatives and involvement

Name vocatives "mark the speaker's involvement with the hearer, co-operation and interest in what is going on in the discourse" (Aijmer, 2013: 37). They function on the discourse level, signaling the speaker's agreement, disagreement, and positive or negative evaluations of the addressee.

Vocatives can signal either agreement or disagreement to the preceding proposition based on the choice of addressing terms. See the following examples:

(2.47) *Xiao Yawen, Ouyang Xue and Ding Yuanying are chatting together*:
肖亚文:丁总,一晃都3年了。
欧阳雪:叫丁总多别扭,你跟我一样叫大哥吧。
肖亚文:好啊,大哥,那我就套近乎了。

《天道》(2006)

(2.48) *He Hongtao brings Xu Sanduo to meet his son Xiaozaizi*:
何红涛:他们是叔叔!…… 你就一个爸爸。今天又给你带回一个叔叔,叫叔叔。
小崽子:(对着许三多)爸爸!

《士兵突击》(2006)

In (2.47), Xiao Yawen initially addresses Ding Yuanying as *dingzong* (boss Ding), showing respect to him and indicating a large power difference. However, when Ouyang Xue suggests that Xiao could call him *dage* (big brother) as well, Xiao expresses her agreement to Ouyang's suggestion by readdressing Ding as *dage*, showing a closer interpersonal relationship. In contrast, when He Hongtao corrects his son the use of *baba* (dad) and asks him to greet Xu Sanduo in (2.48), his little boy still calls Xu as *baba*. Since Xiaozaizi is raised up in the army not only by his father but also by many other soldiers, he develops a false understanding that *baba* is a general title used to address male adults. As a result, even if He Hongtao tries to correct him, the little boy still expresses his cognitive disagreement with his father.

Vocatives also convey the speaker's positive or negative evaluations of the addressee because these addressing terms reflect the speaker's perception of the addressee's social status, personality, and morality. For instance,

(2.49) *Hongye went back and found out that Yin Tianchou has directed one of his underlings to successfully collect protection money.*
洪爷：仇哥，你真行，幸亏了你。
《喜剧之王》(1999)

(2.50) *Guo Yan is arguing with her husband David:*
郭燕：你就是欺负人，流氓。
《北京人在纽约》(1994)

In (2.49), Hongye is impressed with Yin Tianchou's acting talent to collect protection fees and expresses his admiration with a positive evaluative vocative *ge* (big brother) over other general titles. Likewise, in (2.50), Guo Yan is mad at her husband David and addresses him with a negative evaluative term *liumang* (bastard) over other sweet endearments that frequently appear among married couples.

2.4.4 Vocatives and (im)politeness

Finally, vocatives are important in managing interlocutors' interpersonal relationship. Politeness is "concerned with the interactional constraints we follow when establishing, maintaining or breaking interpersonal relationships" (Östman, 1995: 104). Interlocutors apply different addressing terms in accordance with their interpersonal relations. While impoliteness used to be considered as rare in daily communication (Leech, 1983), recent studies have shown that impoliteness also permeates in interpersonal interactions (Culpeper, 2011). This section presents how vocatives are used to convey (im)politeness. See the examples below:

(2.51) *Qiao Zhiyong is asking who is coming and if there is any company. The servant Changshuan replies:*
长栓：翠儿一个人，二爷。
《乔家大院》(2006)

(2.52) *Niu Yuqing and Li Dongbao are chatting about politics:*

牛玉清：太对了，冬宝，就冲你这句话，从此我不拿你当外人。

《编辑部的故事》(1991)

(2.53) *Dong Yunsheng and Ma Jiangwei are fighting wity each other*：
董云升：马江威，我告诉你，你爹充其量也就是一个屁大的官儿，别他妈太嚣张。

《中国的主人》(2008)

In (2.51), by addressing Qiao Zhiyong as *ye* (master), Changshuan manifests their servant-master power dynamic, showing respect to Mr. Qiao. In (2.52), Niu Yuqing uses Li Dongbao's given name to create interpersonal solidarity. In contrast, the name-calling realized in (2.53) violates the social convention in Chinese society and is regarded as rudeness. Nevertheless, the impolite language does not necessarily convey an impolite interpretation. For instance,

(2.54) *Xu Sanduo is showing his father Xu Baishun his military uniform*：
许百顺：反的再来一圈，龟儿子。

《士兵突击》(2006)

In the above example, when Xu Sanduo is about to leave home, his father Xu Baishun couldn't help but swear at him. Instead of conveying rudeness as in (2.53), impoliteness is considered as an exclusive way for the father to show his love to Xu Sanduo.

Finally, it is important to bear in mind that these three pragmatic functions are not mutually exclusive to each other. One vocative could achieve all three pragmatic functions at the same time. See the example below：

(2.55) *Liang Daya saved Han Qiuyun from Japanese soldiers. However, Han is trying to get rid of Liang*：
梁大牙：贱妮子，老子救你，还打老子，不识好歹的东西。

《历史的天空》(2004)

In this example, *jiannizi* serves as an evaluative vocative that first specified the addressee to initiate Liang's complaint; second shows that he blamed Han for not appreciating his help; and third conveys rudeness towards Han Qiuyun. Besides, *jian* can be used separately from vocatives or as an evaluative modifier before vocatives, indicating the extreme contempt for somebody's dishonorable character or way of behavior; and *nizi* is the commonly used vocatives by parents or men of older age in China when showing tender care or pity, something like *sweet*, *honey* in English world—the combination of *jian* and *nizi* uttered by Liang may help convey the subtle feeling of love and complaint intertwined with each other.

2.5 Review

- **Preliminaries**
  - Definition
  - Nature of egocentricity
    - The violation of egocentricity
  - Deictic projection
    - Grammatically determined by addressee
    - Intended to convey additional meaning
- **Deictic and non-deictic uses**
  - Deictic use
    - Symbolic use
    - Gestural use
  - Non-deictic use
    - Anaphoric use
    - Non-anaphoric use
- **Types of deixis**
  - Person deixis
    - Personal pronouns
    - Vocatives
  - Time deixis
    - Time adverbials
    - Tense
  - Place deixis
    - Demonstratives
    - Deictic adverbs of space
    - Deictic directional
  - Social deixis
    - Absolute
    - Relational
  - Discourse deixis
    - Time deixis
    - Space deixis
    - Relative adverbials
    - Topic markings

Chapter 3

Presupposition

In the pilot of the American TV series *Newsroom*, a sophomore from Northwestern University asks the three guests: *Can you say why America is the greatest country in the world?* The first two guests respond to the student with textbook answers such as *diversity and opportunity* and *freedom and freedom*; Will McAvoy, the news anchor who is not satisfied with the status quo, however, points out that America is no longer the greatest country and then gives a rousing speech about how to make America great again. An essential pragmatic phenomenon behind the scene is that the other two guests agree with the student's assumption that America is the greatest country in the world, whereas McAvoy disagrees with it. This implied assumption falls into the study of **presupposition** and will be elaborated on in this chapter.

Section 3.1 and Section 3.2 introduce the two closely related notions of entailment and presupposition. A brief comparison of these two concepts is presented in Section 3.3. The final section discusses the practice of entailment and presupposition in academic writing and interpersonal communication.

3.1 Entailment

Before discussing presupposition, we first introduce the sentential relationship of entailment that concerns the truth condition of utterances. This section begins with the three types of truth and then moves to elaborate on the definition of entailment and its classifications.

3.1.1 Preliminaries

We start this section with three types of truth in philosophical inquiry: *a priori* and *a posteriori*, necessary and contingent, and synthetic and analytic. An ***a priori*** **truth** refers to the speaker's knowledge regardless of the means of acquisition, whereas an ***a posteriori*** **truth** requires empirical testing. For instance,

(3.1) I went to Beijing in 2011.
(3.2) Beihang University has air conditioning for all dormitories.

Sentence (3.1) describes an *a priori* truth because it is the speaker's

Chapter 3
Presupposition

knowledge that he has been to Beijing in 2011. In contrast, whether Beihang University has installed air conditioning for all dormitories needs to be checked on the spot. The second pair is necessary and contingent truth. The mathematical statement *one plus one equals two* is a **necessary truth** because it goes unchallenged in all circumstances. A truth that can be contradicted is a **contingent truth**. For example, the extinction of leaf-scaled sea snakes was a contingently true statement until this type of fish was rediscovered in 2002. The third distinction is between synthetic truth and analytic truth. The **analytically true** sentence is judged from the meaning relations within the sentence, as in (3.3), whereas the **synthetically true** sentence is concluded in reference to the real world, as shown in (3.4).

(3.3) My father is a male.
(3.4) My father is a professor.

To sum up, these differences can be ascribed to the concerns of the analysts: the first set rests on what the speakers know; the second set is a metaphysical one, questioning the nature of reality; the third set is semantically oriented (Kripke, 1980).

Entailment falls into the category of analytic truth and is thus defined as follows (Saeed, 2009: 99):

A sentence p entails a sentence q when the truth of the first (p) guarantees the truth of the second (q), and the falsity of the second (q) guarantees the falsity of the first (p).

This can be presented in the form of a truth table:

(3.5)

p	relation	q
True	→	True
False	→	True/False
False	←	False
True/False	←	True

As seen from the above table, only the truth of the entailing sentence(p) or the falsity of the entailed sentence (q) determines the truth condition of the corresponding sentence. That is, the function of entailment is to predict the truth-value of a statement by referring to that of another. For example,

(3.6) James went to school in Texas.
(3.7) James went to school in America.

Bearing that (3.6) entails (3.7) in mind, if James indeed went to school in Texas, we can also say that he went to America for education since Texas is a state of the U.S. Similarly, when (3.7) is false, one can state that (3.6) is also untenable. Moreover, based on (3.5), we can also derive that the falsity of (3.6) or the truth of (3.7) cannot determine the truth condition of each other. As long as James studied somewhere in the U.S., statement (3.7) remains to be true even if he did not go to Texas. Likewise, if James studied in the U.S. is true, we could not definitively infer that he went to school in Texas.

3.1.2 Types of entailment

Entailment can be dichotomized in three ways: upward/downward entailment, one-way/mutual entailment, and foreground/background entailment.

In terms of direction, entailment is divided into upward and downward entailment (Huang, 2014: 21). An **upward entailment** describes a sentential relation that is from the specific to the general, as in (3.8). In contrast, a **downward entailment** operates from the general to the specific, as in (3.9).

(3.8) a. Children are playing badminton.
　　　b. Children are playing sports.
(3.9) a. Thomas does not like watching TV shows.
　　　b. Thomas does not like watching Saturday Night Live.

Moreover, one may observe that (3.8a) entails (3.8b) but (3.8b) does not entail (3.8a). This type of entailment is termed as **one-way entailment**. A **mutual entailment**, on the other hand, describes entailment that is valid in both directions, as in (3.10).

(3.10) a. Bob is in front of Peter.
　　　 b. Peter is behind Bob.

The distinction between one-way entailment and mutual entailment can be used to examine paraphrasing, which is one of the most common exercises for language learners. A good paraphrase is thus defined as a pair of sentences that mutually entail each other. A poorly paraphrased sentence can be revised through the identification of one-way entailment and its replacement of mutual entailment.

The final distinction is between background and foreground entailments. Our basic grammatical knowledge tells us that most of the sentences include parts of speech such as the subject, the object, and the clause. Each one of these elements gives rise to many background entailments, as in (3.12) to (3.11). According to Levinson (1983: 219), the dichotomy between background and foreground entailments involves a simple pragmatic rule: the **background entailments** of a sentence are considered not closely related to the current context; and when the background entailment is considered adding new information and becoming the point of saying the sentence, it becomes a **foreground entailment**.

(3.11) Tony painted the wall.
(3.12) a. Someone painted the wall.
      b. Tony did something to the wall.
      c. Tony painted something.
      d. Something happened.
(3.13) TONY painted the wall. (stress on Tony)

Sentence (3.12) exemplifies four background entailments of (3.11). By stressing on *Tony*, as in (3.13), the speaker asserts that it is Tony who painted the wall, against the assumed background that *someone painted the wall* in (3.12a). It is worth noting that (3.12 b—d) are not the foreground entailments of (3.13). If the stress is on *painted*, as in (3.14),

(3.14) Tony PAINTED the wall. (stress on painted)

then we can say that (3.14) foreground-entails (3.12 b). Utterance (3.14) is considered as the answer to the question *Tom did what to the wall?*

To sum up, all sentences have a number of entailments—other sentences which are automatically true if the original sentence is true. Entailments are inferences that can be drawn solely from our knowledge about the semantic relationships in a language. This knowledge allows us to communicate much more than we actually say.

3.2 Presupposition

After getting familiar with entailment, we move to illustrate presupposition. This section focuses on its definition, its classifications, its properties, and the main types of presupposition triggers.

3.2.1 Preliminaries

While entailment predicts the truth-value of a sentence via the truth condition of another, **presupposition** describes the piece of information that is presumed to be true for another sentence. For instance, (3.15b) is considered to be true before uttering (3.15a):

(3.15) a. Tony's brother is lovely.
      b. Tony has a brother.

This semantic understanding of presupposition is usually credited to the philosophers Gottlob Frege (1892) and Peter Strawson (1950).

A pragmatic interpretation, on the other hand, attributes presupposition to the speaker rather than the sentence itself. Our real-life experience teaches us that we do not need to state everything in one utterance. For example,

(3.16) *Before leaving for school, Tom said to his mother:*
   a: I am going to school.
   b: I am going to Beijing No. 4 High School today.

Utterance (3.16a) appears to be sufficient to convey the intact meaning in this context. Tom does not need to specify the name of the school because he assumes his mother, the addressee, clearly knows which school he is going to. In addition, following the nature of egocentricity discussed in Chapter Two, it is also redundant for the speaker to clarify that he is going to school on the same day he utters that sentence. The choice of (3.16a) over (3.16b) is dubbed as the **Maxim of Common Presupposition**. That is, a presupposition is the speaker's anticipation of the interlocutors' shared knowledge and is thus left unsaid, achieving an optimal balance between the interlocutors' efforts and the necessary information required by the conversation (Xiang, 2017). Prior to uttering a sentence, the speaker has assumed some mutual knowledge (or common ground) that is appropriate in the corresponding context. For example, the shared information in (3.17b) is the presupposition of (3.17a).

(3.17) a. Tony was late for the party because his car broke down.
   b. Tony has a car.

This common ground could vary cross-culturally. For example, Mey (2001: 145) notes that, in France, asking the storage of oysters normally presupposes that the speaker intends to order some, whereas this presupposition does not stand in America. It appears normal for someone to ask the price of a product without expressing the intention of ordering it. In addition, it is worth noting that mutual knowledge is the hearer's assumption of what the speaker intends him to hold. However, the speaker's statement needn't necessarily correspond to the reality so long as it convinces the hearer of the truth. Conversely, the hearer's responsibility is to identify the intended truth the speaker conveys.

3.2.2 Types of presupposition

Presupposition can be classified into six types: existential, lexical, factive, non-factive, structural, and counterfactual presuppositions (Yule, 1996: 30).

The first important type is **existential presupposition**, indicating that the speaker assumes the existence of the entities named. It is often realized via possessive constructions (e.g., her computer, John's wife) and definite noun phrases (e.g., the President of the United States, the headmaster, the boy on the second floor, the Forbidden City).

Chapter 3
Presupposition

(3.18) John's wife went to Beijing for a conference.

(3.19) The President of the United States held a summit with the North Korean leader in Singapore.

Example (3.18) presupposes the existence of a woman who has marital relationship with John, and (3.19) presupposes the existence of a person who is the President of the United States and another the leader of North Korea.

Another type is lexical presupposition. In general, the identification of **lexical presupposition** is relevant to the conventional interpretation of lexical items. A typical example is the use of *to manage*:

(3.20) a. Yuki *managed* to run a full marathon.
b. Yuki did not *manage* to run a full marathon.

Example (3.20a) implies that Yuki successfully finished a full marathon, whereas (3.20b) suggests that Yuki failed to complete the marathon. It is possible that she might not feel well on the way and had to quit in the middle or she did not run at all. In both cases, however, one can easily draw a conclusion that Yuki tried to run this marathon for a while, and it is thus considered as its lexical presupposition.

While in lexical presupposition, the speaker's choice of a particular expression presupposes an unsaid meaning, a **factive presupposition** indicates the truth of the subsequent information (Yule, 1996: 28). For example,

(3.21) a. Everyone knows that he is gay.
b. He is gay.
(3.22) a. Ben regretted closing the door.
b. Ben closed the door.
(3.23) a. Xiaohui realizes that writing a book is a huge challenge.
b. Writing a book is a huge challenge.

In each example, sentence *a* presupposes sentence *b*. One can *know* something only when it is a fact and people can only *regret* doing something when it has already been done. When a person realizes something, he or she usually discovers a fact. This type of triggers includes *know*, *regret*, *realize*, *be sorry that*, *be indifferent that*, *be aware of*, *be glad/ pleased/ sad that*, etc.

The information following non-factive attitude verbs/ predictive verbs/ mental-process words (such as *dream*, *imagine*, *be likely that*, *suppose*, *pretend*, etc.) cannot be treated as a fact and is described as a non-factive presupposition. To put it succinctly, a **non-factive presupposition** is one that is assumed not to be true. The non-factive attitude verbs block the presuppositions of the embedded clauses. See the examples below:

(3.24) a. I *dreamed of* going to outer space.

    b. I have not gone to outer space.
(3.25) a. Jason *imagined* spending time in Eden.
    b. Jason did not spend time in Eden.
(3.26) a. He *pretends* to be an astronaut.
    b. He is not an astronaut.

In (3.24)—(3.26), the first sentences form a non-factive presupposition with the second sentences. If someone *dreams of* something, he is definitely thinking of something he does not have. And an imagined scenario is nevertheless distant from reality. In (3.26), a real astronaut will not otherwise pretend to be one.

In addition to words or phrases, certain sentence structures also give rise to presuppositions and are termed **structural presuppositions**. The *wh*-question construction is conventionally interpreted with the presupposition that the information under the *wh*-form is true. For instance,

(3.27) Why did you hurt me?
(3.28) Where does Mark keep his money?
(3.29) When did Dillon marry his wife?

Examples (3.27)—(3.29) show that the clauses governed by *wh*-form are structural presuppositions. By saying (3.27), the speaker claims that the addressee has already hurt him. In (3.28), by asking the whereabouts of the money, the speaker assumes that Mark keeps some money secretly. By asking the time of Dillon's marriage, one can work out that the speaker has already known Dillon is married. Apart from *wh*-construction, comparative also produces structural presupposition, as in (3.30):

(3.30) Jennifer is a *better* driver *than* Xiaohui. ≫ Xiaohui is a driver.

Finally, certain linguistic structures can also give rise to a **counter-factual presupposition**, presupposing the absolute opposite of reality. In comparison with non-factive presupposition, what the speaker assumes in counter-factual cases holds a binary relation with the truth. For example, as in (3.26), not being an astronaut is not the opposite of doing other jobs, such as being a student or a teacher. In (3.31), however, the statement that the speaker is the addressee directly contradicts the fact that "you" and "I" can never refer to the same person in the real world.

(3.31) If I were you, I would definitely go to that movie.

3.2.3 Properties of presupposition

Presupposition exhibits two fundamental properties, namely, constancy under negation and defeasibility. Certain cases of defeasibility will cause the

Chapter 3
Presupposition

projection problem.

The first property is **constancy under negation**: in general, a presupposition can survive under negation. That is, if the presupposition of A is true, then the presupposition of *not* A remains to be true. For example,

(3.32) a. Xiaohui's boyfriend is handsome.
b. Xiaohui's boyfriend is not handsome.

Both two sentences in (3.32) presuppose Xiaohui has a boyfriend. Prior to making this judgment, the speaker must have known a person who is the boyfriend of Xiaohui. However handsome this person is, we cannot deny his existence, hence constituting an existential presupposition. This property is a diagnostic test for presuppositions, and is thus dubbed as the **negation test** (Huang, 2014: 89—90).

Now consider the classic example offered by Bertrand Russell (1905):

(3.33) a. The present King of France is bald.
b. The present King of France is not bald.

We may draw a conclusion from (3.33) that there is a person who is the King of France. However, this goes against our common knowledge that the monarchy has been abandoned in France in 1875. This gives rise to the second property of defeasibility. What we listed in 3.2.2 are potential presuppositions (Yule, 1996) and can be **canceled** or **defeated** if they are inconsistent with background assumption, pragmatic inference, semantic entailment, and discourse contexts (see Gazdar, 1979; Huang, 2014: 90; Levinson, 1983: 190).

First, presupposition can disappear when it goes against the interlocutors' background assumption or common knowledge of the world. For example,

(3.34) Tony received an offer from Harvard University before he graduated from Beihang University.
(3.35) Tony passed away before he graduated from Beihang University.

One can easily work out a presupposition that Tony graduated from Beihang at last in (3.34) but not in (3.35). Our real-world knowledge tells us that human beings can do nothing after death. Therefore, Tony cannot finish his degree at Beihang University after his death, and this presupposition is thus canceled.

Presupposition can also evaporate when contradicting with pragmatic inference (which is called conversational implicature and will be further discussed in the next chapter). See the example below (adapted from Huang, 2014: 91):

(3.36) If Mary is organizing a slumber party, Catherine will be angry that she is doing so.

The use of factive predicate *angry* in (3.36) generates a potential presupposition that Mary is organizing a slumber party. The use of the conditional structure *if*, on the other hand, produces a pragmatic inference that Mary is not organizing a slumber party. The pragmatic inference overrides the potential presupposition, canceling the assumption that Mary will hold a slumber party.

In addition, semantic entailments can also cancel the potential presuppositions, especially in the case of negation. For example,

(3.37) The emperor of China can have many concubines, but the monarchy has been abolished since 1911.

In the above example, the first clause presupposes the existence of a person who is the emperor of China and he can marry a lot of concubines. The second half of the sentence, however, entails that no one is the emperor of China since the metric system has been repealed a century ago. Under this circumstance, the entailment takes priority and hence defeats the presupposition.

Finally, presupposition can be defeated when put in a larger discourse. For instance,

(3.38) 听说了吗？村上春树今年终于不用陪跑诺贝尔文学奖了！因为今年诺贝尔文学奖直接取消了。

《北美留学生日报》2018.05.04

The first half of (3.38) constitutes an existential presupposition that there exists a Nobel Prize for Literature in 2018. Our real-world knowledge tells us that Mr. Murakami Haruki has been fortunately nominated for the prize many times but sadly did not win any of them. The combination of the above two elements leads us to an inference that Mr. Haruki must have won the prize this year. The second half of the report, however, stated that the prize in 2018 has been canceled, defeating the existential presupposition we just assumed. What an unfortunate Nobel hunting journey for Mr. Haruki!

From the above analyses, one may observe a dialectical relationship between the above two properties: on the one hand, presupposition can survive when the meaning of the sentence is altered, as in the cases of constancy under negation; on the other hand, some presuppositions will be cancelled such as the cases presented under defeasibility. That is, "how the presuppositions required by a complex sentence relate to the presuppositions required by its component clauses" (Stalnaker, 1973: 454—455)? This compositional issue is referred to as the **projection problem** and has been dubbed as "the curse and the blessing of modern presupposition theory" (Beaver, 2001: 13).

The precursor to handle the projection problem is Lauri Karttunen (1973). He distinguished three types of complementizable predicates: plugs, holes, and filters. **Plugs** block off all the presuppositions of the complement

Chapter 3
Presupposition

sentence. Common examples include *say, mention, tell, ask, promise, warn, request, order, accuse, criticize, blame*, etc. Take *say* as an example:

(3.39) Tom says that Jack's car broke down. But Jack doesn't even have a car!

By using *say*, the speaker merely reports what has been said and does not necessarily commit himself to the same belief. As shown in (3.39), the speaker holds the opposite belief against Tom that Jack does not own a car.

In contrast, **holes** are the predicates that allow all the presuppositions of the complement sentence to survive in the matrix sentence. Representative examples are *now, regret, understand, surprise, be significant, begin, stop, continue, manage, avoid, be able, be possible, force, prevent, hesitate, seem*, etc. If the main predicate is a hole, then all the presuppositions of the component clauses survive. Compare (3.39) with (3.40),

(3.40) Tom knows that Jack's car broke down. *But Jack doesn't even have a car!

It appears to be anomalous to falsify Tom's statement that Jack's car broke down because in uttering *knows*, the speaker commits himself to Tom's belief that Jack possesses a car. If the speaker does not believe that Jack has a car, he cannot verify Tom's claim and therefore should not use *know* to report. Instead, the speaker would opt to *say*.

Finally, **filters** refer to the predicates that could cancel some of the presuppositions of the complement under certain circumstances. The conditions of their usage are proposed in Karttunen (1973) and summarized in Huang (2014: 101):

a. In a sentence of the form "if p then q", the presuppositions of the parts will be inherited by the whole unless q presupposes r and p entails r.
b. In a sentence of the form "p & q", the presuppositions of the parts will be inherited by the whole unless q presupposes r and p entails r.
c. In a sentence of the form "p or q", the presuppositions of the parts will be inherited by the whole unless q presupposes r and p entails r.

And these three scenarios are exemplified in (3.41) — (3.43) respectively:

(3.41) a. If the government promotes that policy, then they will regret doing so.
b. If Snowden returns to America illegally, then he will be arrested.
(3.42) a. James has three children, and all his children are doctors.
b. James has three children, and he regrets not learning art in childhood.
(3.43) a. Either the US government will cancel their meeting with North Korea, or they will regret doing so.

b. Either Snowden returns to America illegally, or he will escape to Russia.

Example (3.41a) is blocked because *they will regret doing so* presupposes that the government will promote that policy, while the first clause entails the same proposition; in (3.41b), the presupposition *Snowden stayed in America before* survives in the whole sentence. As for conjunctions in (3.42), *James has children* is presupposed by the second half of sentence a and entailed by its first half. Therefore, sentence a entails or asserts that James has children. In (3.42b), the same presupposition still survives in the whole sentence under the negation test. Finally, in the case of disjunctions, the embedded presupposition will not percolate up to the whole sentence in (3.43a) but in (3.43b).

This filter-satisfaction analysis, nevertheless, is flawed at some level. As noted by Karttunen (1973: 175) himself, one exception is that the proposition cannot be canceled when the subject of the sentence is the speaker himself, i.e. the subject is I, and the sentence is uttered in the present simple tense. This is rather intuitive in that a person can hold only one belief towards the same issue. And he would report his previous opinion in the past tense if he changed his attitude. For instance, Levinson (1983: 196) points out that some embedded presuppositions can go through the plug, e.g., *say*:

(3.44) Churchill said that he would never regret being tough with Stalin.

In the above case, one can still work out the presupposition that Churchill was tough with Stalin. In addition to this filter-satisfaction analysis, one can also refer to the updated theories of cancellation analysis (Gazdar, 1979) and accommodation analysis (Heim, 1983, 1992).

3.2.4 Presupposition trigger

From the above discussion, we may notice that a potential presupposition is usually triggered by certain words or particular structures. In this final section, following Levinson (1983: 181), we map out the commonly observed 13 types of **presupposition triggers** (see other classifications in Huang, 2014: 86−87, Karttunen, 1974, and Saeed, 2009: 107). The presupposition triggers themselves are italicized; the symbol ≫ stands for "presupposes".

① Definite descriptions (adapted from Strawson, 1950)
E.g., *his car*, *your purse*, *the man*
(3.45) *His son* didn't see *the man* in the red coat.
≫ There exists a man dressed in the red coat.
≫ The man has a son.

Chapter 3
Presupposition

② Factive verbs or adjective phrases
E.g., *regret*, *realize*, *be aware that*
(3.46) Nick Fury *regrets* initiating the Avengers project.
≫ Nick Fury initiated the Avengers project.

③ Implicative verbs
E.g., *manage*, *forget*, *happen to*
(3.47) Xiaohui *happened to* meet Professor Xiang on the street.
≫ Xiaohui did not expect to meet Professor Xiang on the street.

④ Change of state verbs
E.g., *stop*, *finish*, *begin*, *start carry on*, *arrive*, *come*
(3.48) Mary *stopped* jogging after the accident.
≫ Mary used to jog before the accident.

⑤ Iteratives
E.g., *restore*, *rewrite*, *again*, *any more*, *as back to*.
(3.49) Mark *rewrote* the letter.
≫ Mark had written a letter before.

⑥ Verbs of judging
This is not strictly considered as presupposition because the implication is not attributed to the speaker but the verb itself (see Wilson, 1975; Levinson, 1983: 182)
E.g., *accuse*, *charge*
(3.50) He *accused* her of forgery.
≫ He thinks forgery is bad.

⑦ Adverbial clauses of time
E.g., *before*, *after*
(3.51) *After* losing his leg in the car accident, he became grumpy.
≫ He lost his leg.

⑧ Cleft sentences
E.g., "It is ... that/ who" and "What ... is..."
(3.52) *It is* John *that* hurts her.
≫ Someone hurts her.
(3.53) *What* I cared about *was* the holiday.
≫ I cared about something.

⑨ Comparisons and contrasts
They are usually marked by particles such as *too*, *back*, *in return*, or by comparative constructions.
(3.54) Tony donated a lot of money, *too*.
≫ Someone other than Tony donated a big sum of money.

(3.55) John bought a *larger* house.
≫ John already has a house.

⑩ Non-restrictive attributive clauses
(3.56) Tom, *who won three competitions*, is very proud of himself.
≫ Tom has won three competitions.

⑪ Counterfactual conditions
(3.57) If he *were* alive, he would not give up any opportunity to study.
≫ He is not alive.

⑫ Questions
(3.58) Is there a pen here?
≫ There is or is not a pen here.

⑬ Implicit clefts with stressed constituent (also called marked stress)
(3.59) Pragmatics is or is not first systematized by Stephen Levinson.
≫ Someone first systematized pragmatics.

3.3 A comparison between entailment and presupposition

At first glance, entailment and presupposition both indicate automatic relations that interlocutors can work out the truth-value of one sentence based on that of the other. And background entailment can also be counted as presupposition (Levinson, 1983). A close comparison, however, shows that they are different in terms of three properties.

First, interlocutors hold presuppositions, whereas sentences intrinsically have entailments. This distinction gives rise to the second distinction of defeasibility. Presuppositions can be considered as wild guesses the speaker upholds and these general presumptions will be gradually narrowed down to the actual background assumptions the speaker assumes. That is, presuppositions are cancellable when the interlocutors are trying to figure out each other's meaning. In contrast, a semantic entailment cannot be defeated because it is what the language itself conventionally conveys. This fixed sentential relationship comes from stable semantic relations, such as hyponym or synonym. For example, one cannot deny *playing basketball* is *playing sports* because these two phrases form a hyponym. This has nothing to do with the speaker's assumption and cannot be canceled[①]. Finally, presupposition can

---

① While the semantic range of a particular word is fixed **synchronically** (at the same time period), it may change **diachronically** (overtime). For example, the word *bird* used to mean a young bird in particular, whereas the word *fowl* once denoted the same meaning as what *bird* does today (Poole, 1999: 125).

Chapter 3
Presupposition

survive under negation but entailment cannot because the former exists prior to the utterance, whereas the latter coexists with the utterance. A detailed comparison is presented in the table below:

(3.60)

Items	Entailment	Presupposition
Definition	Something logically follows from what is asserted in the utterance.	Something the speaker assumes to be the case prior to making an utterance.
Defeasibility	Cannot be cancelled.	Can be cancelled in a specific context.
Definiteness	Absolute.	Relative.
Function	To predict the truth condition of the entailed sentences.	To infer the potential assumption the speaker holds.
Truth Condition	Suppose A entails B: If A is true, B is true; If A is false, B is true or false.	Suppose A presupposes B: If A is true, B is true; If A is false, B is still true.

3.4 Applications: Entailment and presupposition in real life

As seen from the above discussions, one can find two contrasting functions of entailment and presupposition in language use. On the one hand, strictly following them help readers or listeners to reduce redundancies, avoiding the information that has already been presupposed. On the other hand, the defeasibility of presupposition permits flexible interpretations of the utterances so as to help hearers/readers comprehend the communicative intentions of the speaker. The first half of this section illustrates how the practice of entailment and presupposition contributes to better English writing. The second half interrogates the strategic practices of presupposition in interpersonal communication.

3.4.1 English writing

Concision is essential in English writing. Struck and White (1999: 23) posit that "[v]igorous writing is concise. A sentence should have no unnecessary words, a paragraph no unnecessary sentences, for the same reason that a drawing should have no unnecessary lines and a machine no unnecessary parts." Pinkham (2000) spends a huge chunk of her book discussing the revision of unnecessary words discovered in Chinese-English translations. In this part, we exemplify how entailment and presupposition shed light on the reduction of unnecessary words. The redundant parts are italicized in the following examples.

First, if two phrases form a mutual entailment, the writer can delete either phrase. For example,

(3.61) *He* is a *man* who takes good care of the family.
(3.62) These problems can be easily *solved* and *tackled*.

In (3.61), the pronoun *he* forms a mutual entailment with *man* and therefore is redundant. Likewise, *solved* and *tackled* mutually entail each other. One cannot say something is tackled unless it is solved. In both cases, the writer can choose to omit either word, mostly the longer one, to reach concision.

Second, if two phrases form a one-way entailment, one can keep the entailed part and omit the entailing word. The identification of one-way entailment can improve the precision of the sentence.

(3.63) *My father* is a *man* who takes good care of the family.
(3.64) The government's budget is *good* and *economical*.

Different from (3.61), sentence (3.63) holds a one-way entailment that *my father* entails *man*. The more specific word *my father* should be kept and the sentence can be revised into *My father takes good care of the family*. In (3.64), *economical* entails *good* and thus the latter can be deleted.

Third, a major source of redundancy stems from the failure of recognizing presuppositions. Writers need to identify the potential presuppositions generated by the main idea and reduce the parts that coincide with these presuppositions. The two representative examples are *there be* and *the fact that*:

(3.65) *There are* five students sitting in the classroom.
(3.66) No one realizes *the fact that* Tom is married.

In (3.65), the definite description of *five students* presupposes the existence of five students. It is unnecessary to explicitly express their existence through *there are* and thus can be deleted. In (3.66), the verb *realize* generates a factive presupposition that the following statement is a fact. As a result, it is redundant to use the phrase *the fact that* in the sentence. These two examples are merely signposts for the identification of unnecessary words in a sentence. One can refer back to the presupposition trigger discussed in Section 3.2.4 for further scrutiny of his writing.

Finally, it is worth noting that some repetitions are permissible if the speaker intentionally emphasizes one particular part of the sentence. For example, the use of *man* in (3.61) may mean more than the identification of gender, emphasizing the conventional manhood, such as the responsibility to shoulder the family burden. Otherwise, the above redundancies should be omitted.

3.4.2　Interpersonal communication

While Section 3.4.1 analyzes entailment and presupposition at their production end, this section expounds on their receiving end. Firstly, the exploration of presupposition can convey new information so as to form a language trap to achieve a better rhetorical effect, such as being polite (Xiang, 2017). Consider the following example:

(3.67) **Xiaohua**: I happen to have two tickets for *Romeo and Juliet*. Would you like to go with me?
Xiaoli: Thank you for the invitation. But I have planned to go to another movie with my boyfriend.

In this case, the proposal *going to see Romeo and Juliet together*, in Chinese culture, conventionally entails *going to see Romeo and Juliet as a couple* since *Romeo and Juliet* is a romantic movie and is usually watched by couples. Xiaoli observed this entailment and opted to decline Xiaohua's invitation politely: by saying that she has other plans with her boyfriend, she conveys an existential presupposition that there is a person who is her boyfriend. Thus, she is not available for dates. If Xiaohua can identify this presupposition, he will not ask Xiaoli out anymore, avoiding receiving an explicit rejection. In reality, Xiaoli does not necessarily need to have a boyfriend. What she needs to do is to convince Xiaohua that she is in a relationship to decline his offer.

Moreover, a precise differentiation between entailment and presupposition can reconcile the misunderstanding between couples. For example, a girl would be very angry if her boyfriend tells her to drink more water when she is not feeling well. Her boyfriend, however, does not know why his girlfriend is being grumpy. This miscommunication is caused by the failure of recognizing the boy's entailment. From the boy's perspective, "drinking hot water" mutually entails "the most effective treatment". Girls, on the other hand, usually ignore this entailing relationship.

A careful observation could lead to mutual understanding, whereas excessive meticulousness towards presupposition could also backfire. Take the following joke as an example:

(3.68) *Mary saw a slim girl passing by and asked her boyfriend Tom*:
Mary: Do you love the skinny girl who just passed us?
Tom: No, I didn't see any girl and I love you.
Mary: (*pointing to the slim girl behind*) Her.
Tom: No, she is skinny. I love you.

Mary: Are you saying I am fat?
Tom: No, I'm saying that you are slim and I love you.
Mary: Are you saying that you don't love me if I'm getting fat?

In the first two pairs, Tom probably noticed the girl Mary referred to. Facing Mary's inquisition, however, Tom tried to please his girlfriend by denying seeing any girls. Otherwise, even if Tom answers that he doesn't love that skinny girl, it still generates an existential presupposition that there is a slim girl whom Tom actually paid attention to. The first talk exchange is quite successful for Tom. In the second pair, however, Tom accidentally produced a structural presupposition: the comparison between loving his girlfriend Mary and not loving a slim girl. This comparative presupposes that Mary is not slim. Unfortunately, this potential presupposition was captured by Mary and thus annoyed her. In the final round of conversation, to make up for his mistake, Tom clarified that Mary is skinny and he loves her. This is also backfired because it generates another presupposition that Tom loves his girlfriend only if she is slim. Consequently, poor Tom irritated Mary again.

3.5 Review

- **Entailment**
    - Types of truth
        - *A priori/a posteriori*
        - Necessary/contingent
        - Synthetic/analytic
    - Definition of entailment
    - Types of entailment
        - Upward/downward
        - One-way/mutual
        - Background/foreground
- **Presupposition**
    - Definition of presupposition
        - Semantic view
        - Pragmatic view
    - Types of (potential) presuppositions
        - Existential
        - Lexical
        - Factive
        - Non-factive
        - Structural
        - Counter-factive

Chapter 3
Presupposition

- ○ Properties of presupposition
  - ■ Constancy under negation
    - • Negation test
  - ■ Defeasibility
    - • Projection problem (plugs, holes, filters)
- ○ Presupposition triggers
  - ■ Thirteen types of triggers
    - • Definite descriptions
    - • Factive verbs or adjective phrases
    - • Implicative verbs
    - • Change of state verbs
    - • Iteratives
    - • Verbs of judging
    - • Adverbial clauses of time
    - • Cleft sentences
    - • Comparisons and contrasts
    - • Non-restrictive attributive clauses
    - • Counterfactual conditions
    - • Questions
    - • Implicit clefts with stressed constituent
- **A comparison between entailment and presupposition**
  - ○ Definition
  - ○ Defeasibility
  - ○ Definiteness
  - ○ Function
  - ○ Truth-condition

Chapter 4

Implicature

In the popular American TV show *Friends*, when Joey asks his friends about his performance in the show *Mac and CHEESE*, Chandler praises that the lighting is great and Ross exclaims that they can see him on TV and right in front of them at the same time. One can easily infer that Joey is very bad at the show and his friends are just too shy to point it out. In fact, the show is soon suspended in the next episode of *Friends* due to Joey's awful performance. However, one may wonder how interlocutors work out such a negative meaning (Joey's play is awful) based on two positive comments (good lighting and empathetic experience). This "damning with faint praise" (Peccei, 1999: 28) falls into the study of conversational implicature.

In the first section, we interrogate the different types of meaning, unpacking the coinage of the word *implicature*. The classification of implicatures are shown in Section 4.2. Section 4.3 elaborates the classical Gricean theory of conversational implicature. The next section presents the theoretical development in contrast with the classical Gricean theory. The four main properties of conversational implicatures are illustrated in Section 4.5. The final section illustrates the exploitation of the Cooperative Principle in the American sitcom *Friends*.

4.1 Preliminaries

To understand how the audience is able to work out that Joey's play is awful without explicitly stating it, we need to first figure out what the word *meaning* means. This chapter begins with a distinction between natural meaning and non-natural meaning. Then we move on to introduce the coinage of *implicature*.

4.1.1 Natural and non-natural meaning

To unpack the mechanism of human interaction, the British philosopher Herbert Paul Grice (1957, 1969, 1989) observed the generic use of *meaning* that sometimes we mean what we said literally, but more often we mean something more than what we said, which is often different from or unrelated

Chapter 4
Implicature

to our literal sense. Consider the following examples (Grice, 1989: 213 — 214):

(4.1) a. Those spots meant measles.
b. * Those spots meant measles, but he hadn't got measles.
(4.2) a. Those three rings on the bell (of the bus) mean that the bus is full.
b. Those three rings on the bell (of the bus) mean that the bus is full. But it isn't, in fact, full—the conductor has made a mistake.

Our English language sense tells us that the negation of (4.1a) is anomalous, as in (4.1b), whereas that of (4.2a) is acceptable, as in (4.2b). The kind of meaning expressed in (4.1a) is called **natural meaning**: the meaning relation that *x means that p* entails *p*; **non-natural meaning** or **meaning$_{nn}$** is the one that *x means that p* does not entail *p*, as in (4.2a) (Huang, 2014: 28). And the theory of non-natural meaning is summarized in Levinson (1983: 16):

(4.3) S means$_{nn}$ z by "uttering" U if and only if:
a. S intends U to cause some effect z in recipient H.
b. S intends (a) to be achieved simply by H recognizing that intention (a).

The essential property of non-natural meaning is that it is an intention that is achieved solely through being recognized (Levinson, 2000: 13). In contrast to **what is said**, Grice's major concern of human communication falls into **what is implicated**, viz. implicature. A theory of conversational implicature makes an important contribution to an explicit account of how a speaker expresses more than the literal meaning of his utterance (Levinson, 1983: 97).

4.1.2 Implicature and implication

Before elaborating the Gricean theory, it is important to distinguish implicature (to implicate) from implication (to imply) and inference (to infer). The term *implicature* is derived from the Latin verb *plicare* and is coined to distinguish it from its cognate *implication* (Mey, 2001: 45). We use *p* to represent proposition "Aria helps John with his homework" and *q* to represent the proposition "John will buy Aria a gift". The logical relationship between *p* and *q* could be

(4.4) If *p* then *q*.

Implication describes the logical relation that *q* is automatically true if *p* is true, and *q* could be either true or false if *p* is untrue. This logical relationship, however, does not apply to language practices in the real world:

for sentences such as "If Aria helps John with his homework, John will buy Aria a gift", our interpretation usually would be that John will buy Aria a gift if and only if Aria helps him with his homework. As a consequence, the term *implicature* is coined to represent this real-world implication. Similarly, *p conversationally implies q* can be said that *p implicates q*.

The second set of distinctions is between implication and inference. **Implication** refers to a hint or suggestion that is conveyed via the means of language, whereas **inference** is the deduction drawn from evidence (Thomas, 1995: 58). That is, implication describes the speaker's intention while inference addresses the hearer's interpretation. To conclude this section, we emphasize that the Gricean theory attempts to explain how implicatures are engendered and interpreted rather than how inferences are formed (Thomas, 1995: 61).

4.2 Types of implicature

This section offers a brief sketch of the different kinds of implicatures interlocutors may generate[①]. On the first level, one may create either a conversational implicature or a conventional implicature; and conversational implicature can be further dichotomized into generalized and particularized conversational implicatures; finally, the three common types of generalized conversational implicatures are scalar, clausal, and alternate implicatures.

4.2.1 Conversational and conventional implicatures

The first classification Grice (1989) made is between conversational and conventional implicatures. At first glance, these two types of implicatures are both unsaid meaning that the hearers need to work out. A closer examination shows that **conversational implicature** is an additional unstated meaning that has to be assumed to maintain the Cooperative Principle, whereas **conventional implicature** is an additional unstated meaning connected with the use of a specific word and results in additional conveyed meaning in use (Yule, 1996: 44—45). The former is what we will mainly discuss in this Chapter as in the case of Joey, and the latter is shown in the following examples (the lexical items that engender conventional implicatures are italicized):

(4.5) David is old *but* he is energetic.
(4.6) Tom *also* studies very hard.
(4.7) Gary Locke is a Chinese American. *Therefore*, he was very popular when he was the US ambassador to China.

[①] Readers could also refer to the classification between **audience-implicature** and **utterer-implicature** (Saul, 2002).

In (4.5), the logical connective *but* conventionally implicates that the first half of the sentence forms a contrast with the second half of the sentence. And this opposing relationship cannot be defeated regardless of the extra contextual information added. Similarly, *also* in (4.6) conveys a conventional implicature that there is another person who studies diligently. Finally, the use of *therefore* implicates that Gary Locke's popularity is due to his Chinese ethnicity. Other representative examples include *and*, *actually*, *even*, *anyway*, *barely*, *merely*, *besides*, *manage to*, *on the other hand*, *only*, *still*, *though*, *too*, and *yet* (Huang, 2014: 75; Levinson, 1983: 127, see Potts, 2005 for a systematic study).

One may notice that in contrast to the properties of conversational implicature, conventional implicature cannot be canceled. In addition, it is not calculated by the speaker in accordance with any pragmatic principles but rather conventionally fused in the word.

4.2.2 Generalized and particularized conversational implicatures

Grice (1989) also made a distinction between **generalized conversational implicature** and **particularized conversational implicature**. The former refers to the cases in which an implicature is not normally conveyed by what is said, and its creation requires no specific context, as in (4.8). And the latter is defined as those that are generated through a particular context, as in (4.9):

(4.8) This cup of tea is warm.
+> This cup of tea is not hot.

(4.9) **Waiter**: Coffee?
Customer: It would keep me awake all night.
+> The customer doesn't want any coffee.
+> The customer does want a cup of coffee.

In (4.8), without the help of any contextual information, we can easily work out that the speaker conveys an unsaid meaning that the tea is not hot. In contrast, in (4.9), depending on the customer's evening plans, the waiter may interpret the customer's words as asking for a cup of coffee if he plans to stay up to watch the World Cup or declining the coffee if he plans to go to bed early. In addition, some might get confused about the difference between conventional implicature and generalized conversational implicature since they are both engendered out of a specific context. A simple test would be that a conventional implicature could not be defeated, whereas a generalized one can be canceled in particular cases (Grice, 1989: 39). For instance, we can cancel the conversational implicature in (4.8) if we rephrase it as *This cup of tea is warm, and, in fact, too hot*! However, regardless of what we add to (4.5), one can still work out a contrasting relation between David being old and being energetic.

4.2.3 Scalar, alternate, and clausal implicatures

Under the rubrics of generalized conversational implicature, we usually identify three subtypes: scalar, clausal, and alternate implicature (Huang, 2014). In expressing quantity and degree, interlocutors always face a scale of different choices, for example:

(4.10) <all, most, many, some, few>
<hot, warm, cool, cold>
<always, often, sometimes, hardly, never>

Bearing the above scales in mind, the speaker chooses the most truthful and accurate word within the set. Take (4.11) as an example,

(4.11) Some students attend the class in the morning.

By using *some* to describe the number of students attending the morning class, the speaker implicates that not all the students showed up. This type of unsaid meaning is called **scalar implicature**: "when any form in a scale is asserted, the negative of all forms higher on the scale is implicated" (Yule, 1996: 41). That is, *some* implicates *not all*, *not most*, and *not many*, *cool* implicates *not hot* and *not warm*, and *sometimes* implicates *not always*, and *not often*. Some other scales are listed below:

(4.12) <giant, large, medium, small, minute>
(4.13) <n ... 5, 4, 3, 2, 1, 0>
(4.14) <certain, likely, possible, unlikely, impossible>
(4.15) <excellent, good, satisfactory, pass, failed>

Similar to scalar implicature, **alternate implicature** also implicates the negativity of others when a specific form in the scale is used. Different from those of scalar implicature, forms in the scales of alternate implicature have no hierarchy or gradation, as shown in (4.16):

(4.16) <red, orange, yellow, green, blue, purple...>
<Chinese, English, German, Indian, Japanese>
<北大,清华,北航,人大,浙大……>

If something is red, it is not orange, yellow, green, blue, or purple. Saying *Mary is English* engenders an alternate implicature that Mary is not Chinese, German, Indian, or Japanese (ruling out the case of dual citizenship). If James went to Beihang University in 2011, then he could not be enrolled in Peking University, Tsinghua University, Renmin University, or Zhejiang University,

Chapter 4
Implicature

etc. in the same year under the current Chinese Gaokao system.

While scalar and alternate implicatures are triggered by a specific word, **clausal implicature** is engendered by certain sentence structures (constructions) in cases where the propositions do not hold any entailment or presupposition. The choice of a less certain structure implicates that the speaker is unable to identify the truth or falsity of his statements. See (4.17) and (4.18) for illustrations:

(4.17) If John wins the lottery then he will buy a beach house in Malibu.
+> John may win the lottery or he may not win the lottery; John may buy a beach house in Malibu or he may not buy a beach house in Malibu.

(4.18) Tom or Mary has won the national public speaking contest.
+> Tom may or may not win the national public speaking contest; Mary may or may not win the competition.

In (4.17), the use of "if ... then" over "since ... then" conversationally implicates that the speaker is not in a position to form the stronger causal relationship, indicating that he or she does not know if John will win the lottery or buy a Malibu beach house. This is also true for (4.18). The choice of "p or q" over "p and q" conversationally implicates the uncertainty the speaker holds towards the result of the public speaking contest.

Before expounding the Gricean theory of Cooperative Principle, we summarize the meaning-making process we have discussed as follows (cf. Huang, 2014: 77; Levinson, 2000: 13):

(4.19)

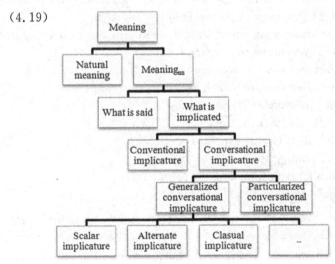

4.3 Classical Gricean Theory

The thrust of Gricean theory was delivered by Paul Grice in the William James lectures at Harvard University in 1967 and was later compiled in his posthumous work *Studies in the Way of Words* (Grice, 1989). This section elaborates on his central idea of the Cooperative Principle and the creation of conversational implicature through strict observation and ostentatious violation of the maxims of the principle. The criticisms of this classical theory are also presented in this section.

4.3.1 Cooperative principle

In order to explain the engendering of conversational implicature, Grice (1975, 1978, 1989) postulates that there is an underlying principle of cooperation that interlocutors will bear in mind for effective and efficient use of language. This principle is labeled as the Cooperative Principle. And following Kant's categorization of objects, it is embodied by four maxims: quality, quantity, relevance, and manner. The principle is shown as follows (Grice, 1975: 45—46):

(4.20) **The Cooperative Principle:** Make your conversational contribution such as is required, at the stage at which it occurs, by the accepted purpose or direction of the talk exchange in which you are engaged.

(4.21) The four maxims:

Quantity
1. Make your contribution as informative as is required (for the current purposes of the exchange).
2. Do not make your contribution more informative than is required.

Quality *Try to make your contribution one that is true.*
1. Do not say what you believe to be false.
2. Do not say that for which you lack adequate evidence.

Relation (Relevance) *Be relevant.*

Manner *Be perspicuous.*
1. Avoid obscurity of expression.
2. Avoid ambiguity.
3. Be brief (avoid unnecessary proximity).
4. Be orderly.

Grice (1989: 28) also notes that other maxims, such as "Be polite", are also commonly observed by participants in talk exchange. Later on, a "Politeness Principle" is systematized by Geoffrey Leech (1983) and will be further discussed in Chapter Six. Moreover, the Cooperative Principle and its maxims are also applicable in non-verbal exchanges. For instance, when having dinner at a restaurant, you expect the waiter to hand you a pair of chopsticks rather than two or three pairs for each person. If you think the soup is too plain, you usually expect the waiter to pass you salt instead of vinegar. And you will not appreciate it too much if the waiter hands you a dictionary when ordering food. And you want the dinner to be served in the order of appetizer, soup, entrée, dessert, and drink rather than backward. These presumptions are the basis for achieving effective communications.

4.3.2 Creation of conversational implicature

Conversational implicatures can be created through either strictly observing or ostentatiously flouting the four maxims: quantity, quality, relation and manner. The creations of conversational implicatures via strict observations are illustrated in (4.22)—(4.25) ("+>" stands for conversationally implicates):

(4.22) *Quantity*
Tom has a son.
+> Tom has at least one son.

(4.23) *Quality*
Stephen Levinson wrote the first textbook of pragmatics.
+> The speaker firmly believes that it is a fact that the first textbook of pragmatics is written by Stephen Levinson.

(4.24) *Relation*
Two students are studying in the library
Jack: When should we go for lunch?
Mary: The library won't close until 11:30.
+> Mary suggests that they should go for lunch after 11:30 when the library is closed.

(4.25) *Manner*
Tom went to the canteen and ordered two dishes.
+> Tom first went to the canteen and then ordered two dishes.

Moreover, the speaker often uses hedges to indicate that he or she abides by the Cooperative Principle and its four maxims. These are shown in (4.26)—(4.29) (the hedges are italicized in the following examples):

(4.26) *Quantity*
a. *As you might know*, Donald Trump is the President now.
b. *To cut a long story short*, Chandler and Monica are engaged.

c. *I may be too wordy*, but everyone needs to bring his passport.

(4.27) *Quality*
   a. *As far as I know*, he is dating Mary.
   b. *I guess* Chomsky is the greatest linguist who is still alive.
   c. *I'm not sure if it is right*, but the left hand is considered to be filthy in India.

(4.28) *Relation*
   a. *I don't know if this is relevant*, but should we talk about the budget?
   b. *This may sound like a dumb question*, but where is the capital of Cambodia?
   c. *By the way*, we will have an exam next week.

(4.29) *Manner*
   a. *This may be quite confusing*, and we should write it down.
   b. *I don't know if this makes sense*, but they spent $200 on a birthday cake.
   c. *I'm not sure if I have made it clear*, but this is the ground rule.

The above illustrations show the creations of conversational implicature through strict observations of the four maxims and the applications of hedges by following these four maxims. Interlocutors, however, may fail a maxim in a number of ways (Grice, 1989: 30): First, the speakers may quietly violate a maxim if they lie without being found out. Second, the speaker can choose to opt out from the Cooperative Principle and its four maxims. For example, instead of directly addressing a reporter's questions, a press secretary could simply state that *I will comment nothing on this issue*. Third, the speaker may face a clash of different maxims. For instance,

(4.30) *Jack does not know the exact place Mary went for the summer vacation*:
   Tom: Where did Mary go last summer?
   Jack: She went somewhere in Europe.

According to the Maxim of Quantity, Jack is supposed to provide the specific location Tom asks for. The Maxim of Quality, on the other hand, dictates that he should not make up the location if he does not know the exact place. Since Jack does not know where Mary exactly went, he is unable to fulfill one maxim without violating the other. Therefore, by answering *somewhere in Europe*,

Chapter 4
Implicature

Jack implicates that he does not know the exact country or city Mary went to for her summer vacation.

Finally, the speaker can ostentatiously flout a maxim, generating a conversational implicature. The exploitations of the four maxims are shown in (4.31)—(4.34) respectively:

(4.31) Flouting the Maxim of Quantity
a. *When Lin Daiyu first came to the Jia family, Wang Xifeng comments*:

"She's a beauty, Grannie dear! If I hadn't set eyes on her today, I shouldn't have believed that such a beautiful creature could exist! And everything about her is so distingue! She doesn't take after your side of family, Grannie. She's more like a Jia. I don't blame you for having gone on so about her during the past few days."

The Story of the Stone (1760/1986)

b. Students are students.

(4.32) Flouting the Maxim of Quality
After his friend lost his iPad, Tom said to his friend:
Tom: You are such a meticulous person!

(4.33) Flouting the Maxim of Relation
A professor is writing a reference letter to a Ph.D. applicant in linguistics:
Tom is a warm-hearted person and he shows up in class on time.

(4.34) Flouting the Maxim of Manner
Waiter: Miss, what can I get you for dessert?
Mary: Ice cream, please.
Waiter: Pardon?
Mary: Ice cream.
Waiter: I'm sorry?
Mary: I-C-E C-R-E-A-M, ice cream!
Waiter: I got it. Here is your ice cream.

In (4.31a), Wang Xifeng flouts the Maxim of Quantity by producing more comments on Lin Daiyu than is required. By constantly commenting on Lin Daiyu in front of the whole Jia family, Wang exhibits her ability to maintain her talking power in a serious setting. This wordiness conversationally implicates Wang's shrewdness and powerful status within the Jia family. In contrast, (4.31b) exploits the same maxim by uttering less informatively. Bearing the underlying cooperation in mind, one has to assume that the two *student*s connotate differently: the second *student* must pragmatically mean something that is embodied by the quality of a student. This tautology may implicate that this student is inexperienced in handling problems. Or this could also implicate that he is diligent and eager to learn from others.

Example (4.32) illustrates the flouting of the Maxim of Quality. Tom's utterance appears to be a compliment to his friends at face value. This, however, happens after his friend lost his iPad, contradicting the characteristics of a meticulous person. This inconsistency gives rise to a conversational implicature that Tom is being ironic to his friend, blaming him for losing his valuable iPad.

The exploitation of the Maxim of Relation can also engender conversational implicature. In (4.33), on a literal level, the professor's reference speaks highly of this Ph. D. applicant in linguistics in terms of his personality and participation. This, although important, is rather irrelevant to the core criteria of a competent Ph. D. applicant, such as good command of languages, sharp analytical skills, and systematic academic training, etc. This divergence from these core criteria indicates that the professor is unwilling to comment on these essential qualities, implicating that the student may be academically incompetent to be recommended as a Ph. D. student. Or at least, the students' academic performance is not salient enough to be complimented.

In case (4.34), the first two pairs of the conversation follow the maxim of manner, viz. to be brief. However, the waiter somehow could not understand Mary very well. Therefore, Mary spelled out all the letters of the word *ice cream*, hoping that the waiter can understand her better. This exploitation of the Maxim of Manner creates a conversational implicature that Mary is irritated by the poor listening of the waiter.

Moreover, non-linguistic cues can also generate conversational implicatures by following or deviating from the underlying norms. For instance, if a thesis is organized in the order of Introduction, Literature Review, Theoretical Framework, Methodology, Results, Discussion, and Conclusions, then, based on the Maxim of Manner, we may work out that the writer is familiar with the basic format of academic writing and is willing to follow it. On the other hand, if the article is organized in other orders, we could implicate that the writer may be unfamiliar with academic writing or at least unwilling to follow suit. For instance, a group of American rhetoricians launched a campaign to try out new ways of writing academic articles in the form of theatric acts (see Powell *et al*, 2014). The violation of the Maxim of Manner, in this case, implicates their unwillingness to conform to the rigidity and their eagerness to make a breakthrough.

Here is an example of how verbal and non-verbal cues jointly contribute to the meaning-making of a communicative event:

(4.35) *A customer ordered one serving of liangpi, a traditional Chinese rice noodle dish mixed with cucumber slices and sesame sauce. During the preparation, the chef cut a huge pile of cucumber slices. The customer saw it and said:*
Customer: No, please do not add too many cucumber slices. I don't like eating cucumbers.
Chef: Well, others still would like to add some.

Following the Maxim of Relation, the customer assumed that what the chef was making was all for his one serving of *liangpi*. Since he saw the cook make a lot of cucumber slices which he didn't want to have, he requested the cook stop making it. The chef, however, did not directly address his request but stated others' need for cucumber slices, violating the Maxim of Relation. This deviation revealed that the slices were not only for this customer but for many customers.

While the above scenarios are generally applicable in many cultures, a maxim could simply be suspended in some cultures such as Malagasy (Keenan, 1976) for the suspension of the first half of the Maxim of Quantity as well as in specific cases of murder, funeral orations, obituaries, poetry, international calls, and jokes (Thomas, 1995: 76-78). In Chinese society, people may suspend the Maxim of Quantity when expressing their affection towards their romantic partner. In Western society, saying *I like you* generates a scalar implicature that the speaker does not love the addressee, whereas in Chinese culture, saying *wo xihuan ni* "I like you" usually implicates that the speaker falls in love with the addressee. This systematic uninformativeness is governed by social conventions.

To sum up, in order to unpack the mechanism of human communication, Grice postulated an overarching Cooperative Principle that interlocutors are consciously observed in conversations. The speaker's meaning or his intention is implicated through the careful observation or ostentatious violation of the four maxims. It is only the maxims that are flouted while this overarching principle of cooperation is still upheld. More exploitation of these maxims in more complex contexts will be analyzed in Section 4.6.

4.3.3 Criticisms of Gricean theory

Positioned as the classical theory of meaning-making, the Gricean theory has been intensively discussed and heavily criticized since its introduction half a century ago (Bach, 1994, 2006; Cao & Xiang, 2017; Gazdar, 1979; Gu, 1994; Leech, 1983; Levinson, 1983, 2000; Recanati, 1989, 2004; Sperber &

Wilson, 1995; Thomas, 1995, etc.). This section presents four criticisms of this classical theory. The reductionist reconstruction of Gricean theory is expounded in Section 4.3 and the expansionist reconstruction will be discussed in Chapter Six[①].

The first problem is that the four maxims are redundant on both the inter-maxim and intra-maxim bases. On an inter-maxim level, Harnish (1976) collapses the Maxim of Quantity and Quality into one single maxim: making the strongest and relevant statement based on the available evidence. Thomas (1995: 91—92) points out that the Maxim of Quantity and Manner seem to co-occur. The first half of the Maxim of Quantity (Make your contribution as informative as is required) entails that the information provided is not obscure or ambiguous; otherwise, the hearer will not be informed properly. Similarly, the second half of the Maxim of Quantity (Do not make your contribution more informative than is required) entails that the utterance is brief. On an intra-maxim level, Mey (2001: 82) argues that the second half of the Maxim of Quality (Do not say that for which you lack adequate evidence) entails its first half (Do not say what you believe to be false). That is, if the speaker does not have enough evidence, he also cannot convince himself that it is false. If I do not study linguistics, I would not be confident enough to think the statement *Avram Noam Chomsky proposed Systemic Functional Grammar* is definitely false (it is actually first systematized by Michael Alexander Halliday who passed away in early 2018).

The second issue is that different maxims may have been assigned with different weights and values. Green(1989: 89) points out that the Maxim of Quality is attached with much greater value than the remaining three values. The violation of quality is considered a serious moral offense, whereas the violation of others is seen as merely inconsiderate or rude. The other three maxims may also be highly valued in different cultural and situational settings. For example, the upholding of the Maxim of Manner is essential in performing a marriage ceremony. In Chinese society, one may be morally prosecuted for being irrelevant when answering the question asked by people with higher social status.

---

① Ideally, we would like to have simple theories that explain a wide variety of issues. In reality, however, scholars tend to prioritize one need over the other when both of them cannot be satisfied properly. The reductionist approach refers to an effort to simplify theories into fewer maxims or rules while maintaining the same level of explanation. On the other hand, the expansionist approach strives to add more maxims or rules to increase the explanatory power of the theory in general. Please refer to Huang (2014) for the reductionist approach and Leech (2014) for the expansionist approach.

The third contention is that the imperative descriptions of these four maxims presuppose a prescriptive nature of the Cooperative Principle. That is, this principle and its maxims are often misunderstood as guidelines for successful communication (Bach, 2005). On the first level, the Cooperative Principle does not appear explicitly as social conventions to an average speaker and thus cannot serve to prescribe interlocutors' behavior. On the second level, contrasting to the universality of the Cooperative Principle proposed by Grice, the assumed cooperation itself can be breached in some cases, notably in conflictive speeches. For example, in military training, the drill sergeant would ignore and interrupt the rookies or even ban them from talking for disciplinary training (Culpeper, 1996: 359). The assumed cooperation is blatantly breached whereas the communicative goal is still achieved. Similar examples can also be found in the practice of rhetoric. For example, Liu and Zhu (2011) argue that speakers should always assume a Non-Cooperative Principle that the addressees will not be voluntarily cooperating with them to achieve their desired outcomes. In addition, persuasion often depends on the hearer's failure of recognizing the speaker's intention by being less truthful (the violation of the Maxim of Quality) and less perspicuous (the violation of the Maxim of Manner) (Dascal & Gross, 1999: 109).

Finally, Grice risked an oversimplification between what is said and what is implicated. It appears to be an impassable gap between the two notions. Our linguistic practices, however, often blur this demarcation. For example, when Usain Bolt says that *he is ready* in front of the starting line of a 100-meter race, he most likely means that he is ready for the race rather than is ready for lunch. Nevertheless, the unsaid words *for the race* obviously will find it difficult to fit in the category of "what is said", and it is also arguably inconsistent with "what is implicated" which requires pragmatic inferences. Therefore, it calls for new sets of principles to separate these notions, and to a larger extent, draw a clear line between semantics and pragmatics. Since then, scholars from diverse backgrounds strive to disambiguate the interface between the said and the unsaid meanings (Bach, 2010; Borg, 2004; Cappelen & Lepore, 2005; Carston, 2009; Chen, 2015; Cao & Xiang, 2017; Huang, 2018; Jaszczolt, 2005; Levinson, 2000; MacFarlane, 2009; Recanati, 2004; Stanley, 2007; Travis, 2008). This book stops engaging this rather philosophical contention with a brief introduction of the two main schools of thought among these debates: Contextualism and Semantic Minimalism. In general, Contextualism scholars advocate that a proposition must go through pragmatic enrichment in relation to contextual information, whereas Semantic Minimalism holds that semantics should be independent of pragmatics, focusing on the most formalized and conventionalized usage (see Huang, 2014 for a review).

4.4 Neo-Gricean and Post-Gricean Theories

This section elaborates on the three main reductions towards the classical Gricean theory. The tripartite proposed by Levinson and the bipartite introduced by Horn are often dubbed as the Neo-Gricean approach and Sperber and Wilson's one overarching principle is called the Post-Gricean approach to conversational implicatures. Let us begin with the most recent advancement in this area.

4.4.1 Levinson's Q-, I-, and M-Principles

Levinson's tripartite was first formulated in 1981 in collaboration with Jay David Atlas and has been developed over the following two decades (see Levinson, 1987, 1991, 2000). The central tenet of Levinson's approach is to establish a clear-cut between pragmatic principles governing an utterance's surface form and those governing its informational content (Huang, 2014: 50). That is, every utterance has a default meaning, and the hearers can work out the intended meaning in reference to that default meaning. Each principle contains a speaker's maxim and a corresponding corollary of the addressee. The simplified set is presented as follows (see Levinson, 2000; Huang, 2014) (square brackets specify their corresponding maxims in the original Cooperative Principle):

(4.36) a. **The Q-Principle** [$Quantity_1$]
Speaker: Do not say less than is required (bearing the I-principle in mind).
Addressee: What is not said is not the case.

b. **The I-Principle** [$Quantity_2$, Relation]
Speaker: Do not say more than is required (bearing the Q-principle in mind).
Addressee: What is generally said is stereotypically and specifically exemplified.

c. **The M-Principle** [Manner]
Speaker: Do not use a marked expression without reason.
Addressee: What is said in a marked way conveys a marked message.

And Levinson (1991, 2000) also assigns different weights to the three principles: The Q-principle enjoys the highest priority, whereas the I-principle obtains the lowest priority. One of the major challenges of Levinson's theory is that it still requires empirical tests to examine the existence of such default meaning (Carston, 2004).

4.4.2 Horn's Q- and R-Principles

Inspired by Zipf's (1949) seminal work on the Principle of Least Effort, Horn (1984) observes two ever-present factors: on the one hand, a speaker has a strong desire to convey his message to others; on the other hand, a speaker is also seeking to spend the least energy to fulfill his needs to communicate. Based on these two competing factors, Horn (1984, 2012) argues that Grice's classification of the four maxims is rather redundant and can be reduced to two principles (square brackets specify their corresponding maxims in the original Cooperative Principle) (Jiang 2000):

(4.37) a. **The Q-Principle** [Quantity$_1$]
Make your contribution sufficient;
Say as much as you can (given the R-principle).

b. **The R-Principle** [Relation, Quantity$_2$, Manner]
Make your contribution necessary;
Say no more than you must (given the Q-principle).

That is, the Q-principle concerns the content of the utterance, ensuring that the speaker offers sufficient information for the addressee to decode; the R-principle, on the other hand, is concerned with the form, dictating the speaker to only produce the necessary information and letting the hearer infer the unsaid meaning.

4.4.3 Sperber & Wilson's Principle of Relevance

Dissatisfied with the four maxims proposed by Grice, Sperber and Wilson (1995) attempt to postulate one overarching principle to account for the generation of unsaid meaning. They contend that human communication works in an **ostensive-inferential** way: the speakers try their best to manifest their intention as clear as possible, and the hearers try their best to infer the speaker's intention based on what the speaker actually says. The speaker's action is called **ostensive communication** and the hearer's move is called **inferential communication**. Sperber and Wilson (1991) also assume that in ostensive-inferential communication, the speaker makes his utterance as relevant to his intention as possible and the hearer infers the speaker's intention based on that assumption. And this assumption of relevance is called the **principle of relevance**: every act of ostensive communication communicates a presumption of its own optimal relevance. However, one major problem is that it is dubious to determine the meaning of "optimal relevance". For example, it would be hard to determine the optimal response to a compliment among "thank you", "I really appreciate it", nodding, and smiling because they are all appropriate responses to a compliment. Since we are unable to determine the optimal relevance, the degree of relevance is also hard to be empirically tested.

4.4.4 Retrospections

The Neo-Gricean and Post-Gricean theories presented above are merely the tip of the iceberg for this core issue in pragmatics, which still bothers and fascinates scholars for further exploration. Although we may be confounded by the abstractness of the individual theory, we can still identify two fundamental research spirits inherited in this line of reasoning, namely, Occam's razor and the identification of nuances.

First, Neo-Gricean and Post-Gricean scholars always bear in mind the spirit of a metatheoretical principle called **"Occam's Razor"** (Huang, 2014: 9). Named after the English Franciscan friar and theologian William of Ockham, the gist of this problem-solving principle is simplicity, and it is also dubbed as the "law of parsimony". For example, iPhone is favored over Blackberry and Nokia is partially due to its reduction from a very complex keyboard to a single Home Button (the latest iPhone X even removes the Home Button) while retaining the similar or even stronger operational efficiency. In linguistic studies, this principle regulates that "senses are not to be multiplied beyond necessity" (Grice, 1989: 47). Therefore, all these three advancements attempt to reduce the original Gricean theory to fewer principles while maintaining similar explanatory power. In Chapter Six, we will expound on the competing expansionist theory, illustrating their justifications for additional maxims and their handling of Occam's Razor.

The second keyword is **nuance**. A closer examination of the classic and new Gricean theories suggests that these different models are not distinct from each other. They all share some similarities: despite differences in details, the Hornian system inherited Grice's Maxim of Quantity, Manner, and Relation and the Levinsonian system maintains Horn's Q-Principle and Grice's Maxim of Manner. To put succinctly, academic advancement is built upon the achievements of the precursors mainly in terms of nuances. In fact, Grice's original theory is widely celebrated precisely because of its strong explanatory power to humans' meaning-making process. The younger generations of scholars identify the shortcomings and propose a new model for the rescue. According to Thomas Khun (1962), scientific study is an iterative process that there will always be shifts of paradigms with the development of science and technology. In our linguistic inquiry, similar shifts happened in terms of the inference pattern of the Relevance Theory to that of the classic Gricean theory and, more significantly, Chomsky's Transformational-Generative grammar to the

Bloomfieldian Structuralism (Harris, 1995: 37).

4.5 Properties of conversational implicature

Conversational implicatures are characterized by a number of essential features among different authors (Grice, 1989; Huang, 2014; Levinson, 1983). In this section, following Grice, we illustrate the four major properties of conversational implicatures: defeasibility, non-detachability, non-conventionality, and calculability[①].

First, similar to presupposition, conversational implicature can be **defeated** or **cancelled** by contextual factors. Take a look at the following examples ("+>" stands for "implicates"):

(4.38) **Xiaohong**: Do you like my hat?
Xiaozhang: It's green.
+> Xiaozhang doesn't like Xiaohong's hat.

(4.39) **Waiter**: Coffee?
Customer: It would keep me awake all night.
+> The customer doesn't want any coffee.

(4.40) **Father**: Have you finished your book report and your housework?
Son: I've done my book report.
+> The boy hasn't done his housework.

(4.41) **Tom**: Are you going to Steve's party?
Mary: Well, Steve's got those dogs now.
+> Mary doesn't want to go to Steve's party.

(4.42) **Mother**: Was the dessert any good?
Daughter: Mom, apple pie is apple pie.
+> The daughter doesn't really like the apple pie.

Examples (4.38)—(4.42) illustrate the conversational implicatures an average interlocutor may infer according to the Cooperative Principle and its maxims. These conversational implicatures, however, can be defeated when further contextual information is added. In (4.38), one may engender a conversational implicature that *Xiaozhang doesn't like Xiaohong's hat* because *lv maozi* "green hat" connotates extra-marital affairs in Chinese culture. This implicature

---

① In addition to these four properties, conversational implicatures may also be characterized by universality (Huang, 2014: 41), indeterminacy (Huang 2014: 42) or implicature changes (Thomas, 1995: 80) and reinforceability (Levinson, 1983: 120; Huang, 2014: 41) etc.

can be canceled if the interlocutors are celebrating St. Patrick's Day in Ireland where everyone wears everything in green or Xiaozhang loves the color of green. In (4.39), the above conversational implicature would be defeated if the customer has to stay up all night for a due assignment. The boy may have finished both works if the father and the son have reached an agreement that the boy always cleans the house before starting to write his book report. In (4.41), Mary would be excited to go to Steve's party if she is a dog lover. The tautology in (4.42) would convey an exactly opposite meaning if the girl's favorite dessert is apple pie.

In addition to adding new information to the existing context, conversational implicature can evaporate via metalinguistic negation. It refers to a way speakers announce their unwillingness to assert something in the conventional way and redress it in a preferred way (Horn, 1985: 135). For example,

(4.43) a. This cup of tea is warm.
+> This cup of tea is not hot.
b. This cup of tea is not warm; it is too hot!
~+> This cup of tea is not hot.

(4.44) a. Peking University is not in Peking.
+> Peking University might be in any other city but Peking.
b. Peking University is not in Peking; it's in Beijing.
~+> Peking University might be in any other city but Peking.

(4.45) *Will McAvoy has insomnia and his girlfriend MacKenzie McHale asks if he has seen the doctor. McAvoy reveals that he doesn't see the doctor but keeps scheduling appointments for the past four years:*
McHale: You have been paying him for four years?
McAvoy: It's ridiculous to say that.
McHale: Thank God!
McAvoy: I have a business manager who does that.
Adapted from *The Newsroom* (2012)

In (4.43), following Grice's Maxim of Quality, one would infer that this cup of tea is not hot; otherwise, the speaker would choose the word *hot* to describe a cup of tea of high temperature. However, the use of metalinguistic negation cancels the conversational implicature that the tea is not hot. Likewise, the conversational implicature generated in (4.44a) disappears when the sentence is negated metalinguistically in (4.44b). In (4.45), *ridiculous* triggers a counter-factive presupposition that Mr. McAvoy did not pay for the appointments for four years. This implicature, however, is soon canceled in the following line when McAvoy stated that he has a business manager who paid the bill on his behalf. Instead of rejecting the payment to the psychologist, McAvoy metalinguistically altered the focus of the utterance, emphasizing the agent who made the payment. What an extravagant lifestyle!

Moreover, conversational implicature carries the property of **non-detachability**. That is, the generation of a particular conversational implicature does not require the sentence to be uttered with specific words. Instead, it is the semantic meaning the sentence contains that invokes conversational implicatures. For example, recalling the previous illustration of the flouting of the Maxim of Quality in (4.32) and restated as (4.46),

> (4.46) Flouting the Maxim of Quality
> *After his friend lost his iPad, Tom says to his friend:*
> **Tom:** You are such a meticulous person!
> +> Tom's friend is not meticulous.

The same conversational implicature can be inferred with the changes of specific words so long as the semantic meaning is maintained, as shown in (4.47)−(4.51):

> (4.47) You are such a meticulous person!
> (4.48) You are such a mindful person!
> (4.49) You are so prudent.
> (4.50) You are very discreet.
> (4.51) You have shown me a very high level of circumspection.

Regardless of the paraphrase, given the context of Tom's friend lost his iPad, one can still work out that Tom is being ironic, implicating that his friend is careless and incautious.

Third, conversational implicatures are **non-conventional** in that it does not belong to the literal meaning conveyed in the utterance (Grice, 1989: 39). Although the creation of what is implicated relies on what is said, there is no necessary correlation between these two concepts. The same sentence may generate very different implicatures in various contexts. For example,

> (4.52) **Tom:** I can't believe that Mary spent $100 on her party.

Tom could mean that he thinks Mary spent too much money on her party if it is only a small gathering of people. On the contrary, if it was Mary's birthday party and she invited a lot of people to the party, Tom may implicate that Mary is very good at utilizing resources. Or he could also intend to criticize Mary for being stingy. All these conversational implicatures are generated by the same sentence. On a diachronic level, however, the distinction between literal meaning and implicature is sometimes blurred. For example, Thomas (1995: 79) notes that the farewell phrase *Goodbye* is a contraction of the Christian catchphrase *God be with you* in the Middle Ages. At that time, a farewell was one of the many implicatures this catchphrase generated. In this modern time, however, the vast majority of English speakers are unaware of its religious origin, taking farewell as its sole literal meaning.

The final feature is calculability. As are suggested in non-detachability and non-conventionality, what is said has little association with what is implicated and would generate many different conversational implicatures. Despite these high uncertainties, interlocutors can still understand each other clearly. This indicates that there must be a certain mechanism that helps hearers to disambiguate the speaker's meaning. And the existence of this mechanism is attributed to the **calculability** of conversational implicatures: the inference is not random in a particular context and can be worked out based on certain knowledge, viz. an educated guess. In general, five types of data are usually required to work out a particular conversational implicature: the conventional meaning of the words used, the Cooperative Principle and its maxims, the context of the utterance, the background knowledge, and the relevant common ground shared by both participants (Jiang, 2000: 59). It is worth noting that the intended meaning may be interpreted distinctively in terms of the speaker's status. For instance, the WeChat "smile" emoji has been widely used in online communication, as in (4.53).

(4.53) 你今天真的太棒了😊

The interpretations, however, display huge differences based on the age of the addresser. When texted by a teenager, it is usually interpreted as a sign of negative evaluation that what the addressee did was far from awesome[①]; if the addressee knows that the above text was sent by a senior citizen, he or she is more likely to stick to a more positive understanding, i.e. the sender was complimenting the addressee on his excellent performance and showing friendliness.

4.6 Applications: Exploiting the four Maxims in *Friends*

In this section, we provide some more analyses of flouting the maxims of the Cooperative Principle in the popular American television series *Friends*. As one of the most-watched TV programs during the turn of the century, *Friends* earned its fame through its outstanding viewer identification and pedagogical implication (Quaglio, 2009) as well as its high resemblance to the accomplishment of everyday social life (Stokoe, 2008). The analyses of these conversations could

---

① See more examples in Huang (2017).

serve as good illustrations of the Cooperative Principle.

4.6.1 Exploiting the Maxim of Quantity

Following the first half of the Maxim of Quantity, one can infer that the speaker's contribution is as informative as what is required. In Season Ten Episode Eleven, Gene and Joey are invited to a popular television game show "Pyramid". They are asked to form a pair to guess the keyword by using other words as hints. They had very bad cooperation for the first two rounds. Now they are in the third and the final round for the big win.

(4.54) *Joey will be guessing and Gene will be offering the hints:*
Gene: Oak, maple, elm, birch...
Joey: I-I-I don't know. Types of trees?
Joey also guessed out the following three keywords:
Gene: Cindy Crawford, Christie Brinkley, Heidi Klum, Claudia Schiffer...
Joey: Oh, oh, oh... (*5 seconds left*)
Gene: Christie Turlington, Kate Moss...
Joey: Girls Chandler could never get?
Gene: (*irritated*) Supermodels!
Joey: Where? (*looking around*)

Friends (2003)

The above example illustrates how Joey worked out or failed to figure out the keywords through the first half of the Maxim of Quantity, i.e. making your contribution as informative as is required. All the words Gene said should be useful to generalize the keyword. Therefore, even if Joey was not very sure, he sensed that all the words are related to trees, and the answer should be something about "the type of trees" (luckily the word is just as simple as Joey's guess). In the final guess, however, he realized the Maxim of Quantity that all these names are necessary to figure out the keyword but failed to recognize the Maxim of Relation when screening his answers: There is no way for Gene and the game show to know Chandler and definitely would not put him as the keyword. Hence, it is important to note that meanings are not always simply inferred from one maxim, but is more likely to be jointly calculated through several maxims.

Interlocutors can also engender conversational implicature by offering more information than is required. In Season One Episode One, Rachel escaped from the wedding and she was really upset. She comes to Monica's apartment for help. Monica's neighbor Joey is also hanging out in Monica's apartment.

(4.55) *Rachel is crying for running away from her wedding and Joey comes to comfort her:*
>
> **Joey:** You need anything. You can always come to Joey. Chandler and I live right across the hall and he is away a lot.
>
> **Monica:** Joey, stopping hitting on her. It's her wedding day.
>
> **Joey:** What. Like there is a rule or something?
>
> *Friends* (1994)

In (4.55), in addition to offering help to Rachel (*You can always come to Joey*), Joey also added an extra piece of information (*Chandler and I live right across the hall and he is away a lot*). By suggesting that his apartment is close to hers, and he has plenty of time of being alone, Joey violated the Maxim of Quantity, creating a conversational implicature that he wants to date Rachel, or at least, to flirt with her. This unsaid meaning, however, is successfully inferred by Monica. As a good friend of Rachel, Monica stopped Joey from continuing doing so (*Joey, stopping hitting on her. It's her wedding day*).

4.6.2 Exploiting the Maxim of Quality

Bearing the first part of the Maxim of Quality in mind, interlocutors can conversationally implicate something by ostentatiously saying what the speaker believes to be false. In Season One Episode Four, Ross accidentally breaks his nose and his friend Chandler is accompanying him in the hospital. Chandler is curious about Ross's recent divorce because his ex-wife turns out to be a lesbian.

(4.56) **Chandler:** What is it? Did she leave you? Did she leave you for another woman that likes women?
>
> **Ross:** A little louder, please. Because I think there is a man on the 12th floor in a coma who didn't quite hear you.
>
> **Chandler:** (*silent*)
>
> *Friends* (1994)

In scenario (4.56), one may notice that Chandler is being very annoying to Ross by constantly asking the whereabouts of Ross's ex-wife. In addition, talking loudly is also conventionally prohibited in the hospital. Since Chandler is his best friend, Ross stops Chandler in an ironic way. By saying that a patient in a coma on a different floor should also hear Chandler, Ross violates the Maxim of Quality in that it is impossible for the patient to hear Chandler's questions. Chandler successfully understands Ross's implicature and stops asking questions, rather than accepting Ross's "suggestion" and speaking even louder.

Corresponding to the second part of the maxim, interlocutors should not say that for which they lack adequate evidence. In Season Two Episode Three, Phoebe and Ross are arguing about the persuasiveness of the Theory of Evolution. Ross firmly believes in evolution, but Phoebe still doubts about it.

(4.57) **Ross:** Uh, excuse me. Evolution is not for you to buy, Phoebe. Evolution is a scientific fact, like, like, like the air we breathe, like gravity.

Phoebe: Ok, look, before you even start, I'm not denying evolution, ok, I'm just saying that it's one of the possibilities... Now, are you telling me that you are so unbelievably arrogant that you can't admit that there's a teeny tiny possibility that you could be wrong about this?

Ross: There might be...a teeny...tiny...possibility.

Phoebe: I can't believe you caved.

Ross: What?

Phoebe: You just abandoned your whole belief system. Now I mean, before, I didn't agree with you, but at least I respected you.

Friends (1995)

In (4.57), Ross states that evolution is a scientific fact. According to the Maxim of Quality, one should not say something without adequate evidence. Therefore, following this maxim, one would easily infer that Ross firmly believes in evolution. Then Phoebe questions him about if there would be a slight chance that the entire theory of evolution is falsely constructed. Bearing the scientific discretion in mind, Ross admits the possibility of alternative explanations. This meticulousness, however, is construed by Phoebe as an abandonment of his belief system: Ross is saying something without sufficient proof, generating a conversational implicature that he does not believe in evolution anymore.

4.6.3 Exploiting the Maxim of Relation

In Season Four Episode Five, after Ross and Rachel break up, Ross finds a new girlfriend whereas Rachel is still single. In the coffeehouse, Ross intends to show off his new girlfriend Amanda to Rachel.

(4.58) *Ross, Rachel, Chandler, and other friends are sitting in the café:*

Ross: Yeah. It's tough being single. That's why I am so glad I found Amanda.

Rachel: Ross, you guys went out once. You took your kids to Chucky Cheese, and you didn't even kiss her.

>   **Ross**: (*Staring at Chandler angrily*)
>   **Chandler**: I tell people secrets. It makes them like me.
>
>   *Friends* (1997)

In the above case, Ross is clearly mad at Chandler for telling his secret to Rachel, ruining his chance to show off in front of her. Instead of admitting his mistake, Chandler makes a general statement about him liking to tell people's secrets for affection. This appears to be irrelevant to Ross's expectation at face value. Bearing the assumption that Chandler is aware of the Maxim of Relation, however, one could work out a conversational implicature that Chandler tells the secret to Rachel that Ross does not enjoy a successful date with Amanda.

4.6.4 Exploiting the Maxim of Manner

Breaching the Maxim of Manner can create dramatic humorous effects. In Season Four Episode Thirteen, Rachel cannot stand the dullness of her job at Bloomingdale's and decides to quit. Before talking to her boss, she calls Monica:

> (4.59) **Rachel**: Monica, I'm quitting! I just helped an 81-year-old woman put on a thong and she didn't even buy it! (*Pause*) I'm telling you I'm quitting! That's it! I'm talking to my boss right now! (*Pause*) Yes I am! (*Pause*) Yes I am! Yes I am! Yes I am! Yes I am! Yes I am! Okay bye, call me when you get this message.
>
> *Friends* (1997)

Since the Maxim of Manner postulates that interlocutors should converse orderly, the pause held between Rachel's monologue generates a conversational implicature to the audience that Monica has responded. This implicated meaning, however, is soon defeated when Rachel says that *Okay bye, call me when you get this message* which presupposes that Monica has not received the message yet. This dramatic cancellation, therefore, creates a humorous effect on the audience.

When addressees fail to identify the exploitation of maxims, they may unable to infer the speaker's intention, causing an awkward communication failure. In Season Five Episode Nineteen, Chandler reveals that Ross is not good at flirting. In order to disprove Chandler's statement, Ross tries to flirt with the pizza delivery girl Caitlin that he likes her and wants to ask her out. See the scenario below:

> (4.60) *In her last delivery, Caitlin said that she thought her haircut looks like an eight-year-old. When Caitlin arrived with a pizza, Ross started to flirt:*

Chapter 4
Implicature

    Ross: By the way, if it makes you feel any better... I happen to like 8-year-old boys.
    Caitlin: What?
    Ross: The uh, your hair, before, your hair, you said you thought your hair looks like an 8-year-old's, and I'm just saying I like it. The hair.
    Caitlin: Oh. Thanks.
    Ross: You understand I don't actually like 8-year-old boys.
    Caitlin: Y' know, all I'm looking for is the money.
    Chandler: (*Handing Caitlin the money*) Here you go. Now stop bringing us pizzas you.
    Caitlin: I'm gonna try. (*Caitlin walks away and Ross closes the door*)

Friends (1998)

Instead of complimenting Caitlin on her hair directly, Ross chooses to express his affection for her in an implicit and rather obscured way. By saying that he likes eight-year-old boys, Ross expects Caitlin to infer a conversational implicature that he likes her by recalling her earlier complaint of looking like an eight-year-old. Caitlin, however, does not successfully identify Ross's implicature and takes his word literally, considering him pedophilic. This miscommunication is a result of Caitlin's failure to recognize that Ross flouted the Maxim of Manner (avoid ambiguity). The second fiasco happened when Ross tries to clarify that he does not like young boys' hair. This time, Caitlin wrongly infers that Ross is trying to deny his affection towards children because an average adult normally does not make disclaimers of being sexually interested in kids. According to Levinson's M-Principle (What is said in a marked way conveys a marked message), Ross must have used this in a marked way, revealing the fact that he is pedophilic. These two miscarriages are due to the poor handling of the Cooperative Principle by Ross and, in turn, proving that he is a green hand of flirting.

4.7 Review

- **Preliminaries**
    - Natural meaning and non-natural meaning
    - Implication and implicature
    - Types of implicatures
        - Conversational and conventional implicatures
        - Generalized and particularized conversational implicatures
        - Scalar, alternate, and clausal implicatures

- **Classical Gricean theory**
  - Cooperative Principle
    - Quality
    - Quantity
    - Relation
    - Manner
  - Creation of conversational implicatures
    - Careful observation
    - Ostentatious infringement
  - Criticisms of the Gricean theory
    - Redundancy within one maxim and between maxims
    - Different weighs of the four maxims
    - Prescriptive nature
    - Oversimplification between what is said and what is implicated
- **Neo-Gricean and Post-Gricean theories**
  - Levinson's tripartite
    - Q-principle
    - I-principle
    - M-principle
  - Horn's bipartite
    - Q-principle
    - R-principle
  - Speber & Wilson's relevance theory
    - Ostensive-Inferential communication
    - Principle of Relevance
- **Properties of conversational implicature**
  - Defeasibility
    - Linguistically
    - Metalinguistically
  - Non-detachability
  - Non-conventionality
  - Calculability
    - Conventional meaning of the words used
    - Cooperative Principle and its maxims
    - Context of the utterance
    - Background knowledge
    - Relevant common ground shared by both participants

Chapter 5

Speech Acts

On May 20, 2018, US President Mr. Donald Trump tweeted the following:

> *I hereby demand, and will do so officially tomorrow, that the Department of Justice look into whether or not the FBI/DOJ infiltrated or surveilled the Trump Campaign for Political Purposes—and if any such demands or requests were made by people within the Obama Administration!*
>
> @realDonaldTrump

This message is seen as a red herring (something that misleads or distracts from the important issue) to the ongoing investigation that Mr. Trump's 2016 presidential campaign has been rigged by Russian influence. By posting this tweet, Mr. Trump urges the Department of Justice to do something or to perform certain acts. His performance of demanding falls into the category of **speech act**. When a series of these performative acts are carried out for the same purpose, it is called a **speech event**. These are considered as the basic or minimal units of our linguistic communication (Searle, 1969: 16).

This chapter is organized as follows: Section 5.1 unpacks the origin and definition of speech acts. Section 5.2 and Section 5.3 introduce John Austin's original theory of speech act and the advancements made by his student John Searle. Section 5.4 highlights some of the latter theoretical advancements along the line of the Speech Act Theory. The variations of speech acts across cultures and contexts are illustrated in Section 5.5. Finally, Section 5.6 presents an empirical study of the persuasive strategies in Chinese online forum requests.

5.1 Preliminaries

To understand how Trump's message performs acts, in the first subsection, we recount the seminal dichotomy between performative and constative; the second subsection introduces the performative hypothesis formulated to remedy this troubling dichotomy.

5.1.1 Performative-constative dichotomy

In the early twentieth century, a group of philosophers led by Bertrand Russell hold that every single statement can be judged to be true or to be false. For example, by going through a metal detector in the airport, one can easily test if the examinee's statement of *I do not bring any metals with me* is true or false. If the metal detector goes off, the TSA officers will know that the passenger's statement is false. Otherwise, the passenger is telling the truth. As for those statements that cannot be tested, these philosophers counted them meaningless. For instance,

(5.1) Captain America plays better chess than Stan Lee.

Statement (5.1) is meaningless because Captain America is fictitious and there is no way to hold a chess match between the two. Consequently, the truth condition of the above statement can neither be proved nor falsified. Those who believe that a meaningful sentence can be verified for its truth-value are called the **logical positivists** (more precisely, descriptive fallacy) and the linguistic approach they adopted is known as **truth-conditional semantics** (see Lyons, 1995: 237). The British philosopher John Austin (1962), however, sharply observes that sentences could do more than making statements. For example,

(5.2) a. Beijing is the capital city of China.
b. Beijing is the capital city of Japan.
(5.3) (Smashing the bottle against the stem) (Austin, 1962: 5)
I name this ship Queen Elizabeth.
(5.4) I ask you to buy some pizza.

In (5.2), one could easily tell that (5.2a) is true and (5.2b) is false based on their geographical knowledge. For sentences (5.3) and (5.4), however, it is hard to tell their truth conditions. We could verify if the speaker named the ship Queen Elizabeth or Prince Philips, but we are unable to say whether sentence(5.3) is true or not. The same conclusion applies to (5.4): we could tell the truth or falsity of sentences like *Tom asked Mary to buy some Pizza*, but not that of (5.4). After identifying these discrepancies, Austin named sentences or utterances like (5.2a) and (5.2b) **constatives** that are used to make descriptions and statements. In contrast, those like (5.3) and (5.4) are dubbed as **performatives**, or **speech acts**: Utterances that are not just saying something but also doing actions. The verbs used to perform these actions, such as *name*, *ask*, and *pronounce*, are called **performative verbs**, and are later dubbed as Illocutionary Force Indicating Device (IFID) in Searle's (1969) term. A sharp reader may notice that some utterances do not have an explicit performative verb as the verb *demand* in Mr. Trump's tweet. This type of performatives is called **primary performatives** (Austin, 1962: 69) or **implicit performatives** (Huang, 2014: 121; Levinson, 1983: 231)①. And those with such a verb is dubbed as **explicit performatives** (Austin, 1962: 32). Some more examples are listed below:

(5.5) Explicit performatives (the performative verbs are italicized)
   a. I *promise* to give gou your money back.
   b. We *suggest* you report to the administration.
   c. I *order* you to surrender now.
   d. I hereby *sentence* you to death.

(5.6) Primary/implicit performatives
   a. I will see you tomorrow at the office.
   b. How about going to the zoo tomorrow?
   c. I'm sorry.
   d. It's hot here.

5.1.2 The performative hypothesis

The observation of implicit performatives might make people wonder how utterances can still trigger actions without an explicit performative verb. This is explained by the theory of the **performative hypothesis** put forward in the 1970s (see Ross, 1970; Sadock, 1974). The central argument is that every sentence contains a "hidden form" that can give rise to explicit performatives (Sadock, 1974: 17); this structure is composed of the speaker as the subject, the addressee as the indirect object, an abstract performative verb (e. g., *promise*, *order*, *suggest*, etc.), and a complement clause specifying the act. The implicit performatives in (5.6) can be rewritten as follows:

(5.7) a. I (hereby) promise you that I will see you tomorrow at the office.
   b. I (hereby) ask you that how about going to the zoo tomorrow.
   c. I (hereby) apologize to you that I'm sorry.
   d. I (hereby) state the fact to you that it's hot here.

This hypothesis, however, was soon abandoned for the grammatical indistinctiveness of abstract performative verbs, i. e., we simply have no idea

---

① The word *primary* is favored over *implicit* because it indicates an evolutionary direction. Viewing from language evolution, the explicit performatives are the later development of some primary utterances; the primitive form retains a degree of ambiguity and is made explicit based on numerous successful communications (Austin, 1962: 71—73).

of their inventory and a lot of verbs could be either included in or excluded from the category (Thomas, 1995: 44; Yule, 1996: 53). And some implicit performatives have no appropriate explicit counterpart, as in the cases of lying, punishing, and threatening (Huang, 2014: 124). For example,

(5.8) a. You are such a pig.
b. * I hereby insult you that you are such a pig.
c. Tony insulted Mary that she was such a pig.

(5.9) a. I promise I will beat you up.
b. * I hereby threaten you that I will beat you up.

The rewriting of (5.8a) in (5.8b) appears to be odd for native speakers, whereas the verb "insult" can be used explicitly in a descriptive manner, as in (5.8c). Moreover, utterance (5.9a) performs an action of threatening but is expressed via the explicit performative verb "promise". The explicit use of "threaten", however, is generally unacceptable.

5.2 Austin's theorizing of speech acts

As the founding father of the Speech Act Theory, John Austin draws wisdom from Wittgenstein's Game Theory and presented his seminal thoughts during his stay at Harvard University for William James lectures in 1955 (Harris, 1995: 126). Following his dichotomization between constatives and performatives, this section presents his felicity conditions on performatives, the three facets of speech acts, and their categorizations.

5.2.1 Felicity conditions on performatives

Since speech acts cannot be tested by truth-value, Austin (1975: 14—15) proposed a set of conditions for politic performatives and named them **felicity conditions**:

(5.10) **A.** (a) There must be a conventional procedure having a conventional effect. (b) The circumstances and persons must be appropriate for the invocation of a particular procedure.

B. The procedure must be executed by all participants (a) correctly and (b) completely.

C. Often, (a) the persons must have the requisite thoughts, feelings and intentions, as specified in the procedure, and (b) if consequent conduct is specified, then the relevant parties must so do.

For example, *I hereby sentence you to death* is only felicitous when it is uttered by the judge in the court during the criminal justice procedure. The violation of any of the above conditions will render the speech act infelicitous. Austin (1962) identified two types of infelicities: first, a **misfire** takes place when conditions A or B are infringed, as in cases where the judge sentences someone's death in the bathroom or the sentence is delivered by a salesman. Second, an **abuse** occurs if condition C is not followed as in that the judge intentionally sets up an innocent person or the law enforcement refuses to execute the criminal. Strawson (1964, 1971) points out that Austin's felicity condition only applies to formal and ritualistic acts, overlooking the huge amount of daily activities where the conditions are not necessary. For instance, when raising money for the charity, fundraisers often think out of the box and create an unconventional way to advocate, violating Austin's felicity condition (Aa).

In modern times, some rituals are even performed outside of their conventional settings. In 2012, a couple from southern Minnesota got married next to their parents' graves to honor them and their family (BMTN staff 2012). In fact, many weddings are performed in mountain sites, farms, bay resorts, seaside, etc. (Wedding Reception Venues near Newry, ME n. d.). Even though these wedding ceremonies were performed in unusual locations, they are still legitimate, contradicting Austin's postulation of felicitous conditions.

5.2.2 Locutionary, illocutionary, and perlocutionary acts

In the course of identifying all possible explicit performative verbs, Austin (1962: 94) realized that performatives and constatives might not be clear-cut. This led him to abandon his early dichotomy and to argue that constatives is only a special subcategory of performatives; thus, all utterances perform some actions. Then he presented a threefold distinction of a speech act: locutionary, illocutionary, and perlocutionary acts. **Locutionary act** or **locution** refers to the utterances with a particular form and a relatively fixed meaning (Lyons, 1995: 240). **Illocutionary act** or **illocution** addresses the functions the speaker intends to achieve or the action the speaker wants to accomplish via locutionary act, such as accusing, apologizing, blaming, commanding, congratulating, giving permission, joking, nagging, naming, ordering, promising, refusing, requesting, suggesting, swearing, and thanking (Huang, 2014: 128). These functions are also known as the **illocutionary force**. And **perlocutionary act** or **perlocution** is the sequential effects the utterance acts onto the interlocutors' feelings, thoughts, or actions (Austin, 1962: 101). These three dimensions are exemplified as follows:

(5.11) The tripartite of a speech act:

> *Locutionary act*: The room is hot.
> *Illocutionary act*: The speaker suggests the addressee open the door.
> *Perlocutionary act*: The addressee walks to the door and opens it.

In the above example, by performing the locutionary act of uttering *the room is hot*, the speaker intends to fulfill the illocutionary function of suggesting the addressee open the door. The consequence is that the addressee walks to the door and opened it. This perlocutionary effect, however, is by no means fixed. It may well be that the addressee thinks the room is cool and refuses to open the door.

5.2.3 Types of illocutionary force

Among the three facets discussed above, illocutionary act or illocutionary force is the one that draws the most attention from pragmaticians. Based on the criteria of true-false and value-fact dichotomies, Austin (1962: 151) grouped illocutionary force into five types: verdictives, exercitives, commissives, behabitives, and expositives. **Verdictives**, as the name implies, give verdicts (fact or value) about the things that are uncertain. Common examples are to acquit, to assess, to convict, to estimate, to find, to rank, to rule, and to value. **Exercitives** refer to the exercise of powers, rights, or influence, such as to advise, to appoint, to beg, to claim, to degrade, to demote, to name, to pardon, to repeal, to urge, to vote, and to veto. Closely connected with verdictives and exercitives, **commissives** commit the speaker to a certain course of action, as in to adopt, to agree, to bet, to contract, to declare, to embrace, to guarantee, to plan, and to promise. **Behabitives** express the speaker's attitude and behavior towards someone else's previous actions, such as to apologize, to bless, to condole, to congratulate, to criticize, to overlook, to thank, to welcome, and to wish. Finally, **expositives** concern our use of words in arguments and conversations, such as to affirm, to answer, to agree, to deny, to mention, to report, and to withdraw.

Austin's theorizing is insightful and illuminating in terms of its challenge to logical positivism[①] and the provision of a solid foundation for the school of ordinary language philosophy as well as the study of pragmatics. While as a cautious person himself, Austin was not a proliferate writer and did not leave

---

① Logical positivism refers to a philosophical belief that the world is composed of facts that can be verified and analyzed based on their truth value. Austin's theory forms a direct contrast because he finds that some statements cannot be explained in terms of truth condition.

too many publications for us to explore. The only book *How to Do Things with Words* was published posthumously based on the recollection of his lectures from his students. Since then, many scholars tend to revise, defend or challenge his theory (e. g. Strawson, 1964; Searle, 1969; Bach & Harnish, 1979; Wierzbicka, 1987; Sadock, 1994). Among them, his student John Searle (1969, 1975, 1979) is unquestionably the most influential one.

5.3 Searle's theorizing of speech acts

In this section, we present Searle's three major advancements in the Speech Act Theory: a new proposal of felicity condition, an updated typology of speech acts, and a theory of indirect speech acts.

5.3.1 Felicity conditions on speech acts

In the last chapter, we introduced Grice's Cooperative Principle and its four maxims to unpack the inferential mechanism of speech acts. Grice's informal approach, however, does not specify the relationship between conventions and the meaning-making process. Furthering Austin's felicity condition, Searle (1969: 63) attempts to come up with a formal approach to speech acts, arguing that to successfully perform a speech act is to obey a set of rules that constitute that act. The table below illustrates Searle's felicity condition for promising:

> (5.12) Felicity condition for promising
> *Propositional content condition*: Speaker predicates a future act of the speaker.
> *Preparatory condition*: Speaker believes that doing act A is in H's best interest and that S can do A.
> *Sincerity condition*: Speaker intends to do act A.
> *Essential condition*: Speaker undertakes an obligation to do act A.

This can be exemplified in the following example: Suppose John says to Mary: *I promise to return your book tomorrow*. The propositional content is that John says that he will perform an act of returning Mary's book in the future time of tomorrow. John also believes that returning Mary's book is in her best interest, and he is fully capable of doing so. Moreover, John utters the sentence in a sincere manner that he really intends to give the book back to her. Finally, in saying these words, John is obliged to perform this act.

The violation of any of the conditions, however, would render the act infelicitous, such as John promises that Tom will return Mary's book (violation of propositional content condition), John lost Mary's book (violation of preparatory condition), John is lying (violation of sincerity condition), or Mary says that

John does not have to return the book (violation of essential condition). One may find many occurrences of infelicitous acts in our real lives, as shown in (5.13)—(5.15).

(5.13) *When seeing a nice purse, Xiaowang says to her boyfriend.*
Xiaowang: I don't want that purse.

(5.14) *Tom irritates John with four-letter words.*
John: Say that again!

(5.15) *The father finds his son is playing computer games:*
Son: I promise I'll start to do my homework in five minutes.

Anyone who has experiences in a romantic relationship can easily tell that (5.13) actually means that Xiaowang wants that new purse. Tom would not dare to curse John again for the sake of their friendship because he knows that John's act is infelicitous. The little boy in (5.15) is very unlikely to do his homework when the five-minute countdown ends because he does not really intend to do so, breaching the sincerity condition.

The above analyses show that it is possible to establish a set of constitutive rules to account for the nature of all speech acts, mending Austin's over-emphasis on institutionalized speech acts. Searle (1969: 66—67) also lists felicity conditions for eight more illocutionary acts, including requesting, asserting, questioning, thanking, advising, warning, greeting, and congratulating. Searle's ambitious proposal, however, remains problematic in that it is unable to clearly distinguish all speech acts and it sometimes filters out the perfectly normal speech acts, leaving some other odd cases unaddressed (Thomas 1995: 95). For instance, the popular slogan of the movie *Star Wars* "May the Force be with you" does not fit into any of Searle's categories.

5.3.2 Typology of speech acts

In classifying speech acts, Austin (1962: 151) was not satisfied with his own categorizations and their recondite names. Searle (1979: 10) points out that the biggest weakness of Austin's taxonomy is that it has no clear and consistent principle to be rooted in. Consequently, the original classification exposes confusions between performatives and performative verbs and overlapping between different categories.

To address the shortage of governing principles, Searle (1979: 2—12) identifies 12 significant dimensions of variation for different speech acts, among which the most important three are the illocutionary point, the direction of fit, and the expressed psychological states. **Illocutionary point** is the essential condition of a speech act. The illocutionary point of order is to get the addressee to do something, whereas that of a promise is to oblige the speaker himself to do something. **Direction of fit** concerns the matching relation between the words and the world. For example, a customer's shopping list is to get the groceries in the world to fit the required items on the list, whereas a cashier's receipt is to let the words on the receipt fit the items the shopper actually bought in the world (c. f. Anscombe, 1957). Finally, the **expressed psychological states** refer to the speaker's attitude or state to that propositional content, as in one's desire in a request, one's belief in an order, and one's intention in a promise.

Bearing the above dimensions in mind, Searle (1979) presents his fivefold typology of speech acts: assertives, directives, commissives, expressives, and declarations.

Assertives or **representatives** commit the speaker to something to be the case with a testable truth condition. In uttering an assertive, the speaker makes words fit the world, expressing the psychological state of belief. Representative examples include statements of facts, assertions, conclusions, and descriptions, as shown in (5.16)—(5.19) respectively.

(5.16) Beijing is the capital city of China.
(5.17) Usain Bolt is the fastest sprinter.
(5.18) The paper concludes that Searle's theory is self-contained.
(5.19) John is bald.

However, one needs to be conscious that the truth or falsity of an assertive is not clear-cut. In example (5.19), we usually consider a person bald even if he still has a few hairs left. Similarly, we do not take it as a false statement in our daily life if someone says that China now has 1.4 billion people (the actual number is 1,414,578,727 by May 20, 2018) (World Population, 2018).

The illocutionary point of a **directive** is to get the hearer to do something. In so doing, the speaker expresses his desires or wants, fitting the world to words via the addressee. Typical examples are suggestions, invitations, requests, and orders, as shown in (5.20)—(5.23).

(5.20) It would be better to wear in layers at the turn of seasons.
(5.21) Could you join us for John's party?
(5.22) A cup of black coffee, please.
(5.23) Attention! (Said by the drill sergeant to the rookies)

Directives are tightly connected to the study of politeness. In general, interlocutors tend to apply various pragmatic modifiers (e. g., could, would, please) to redress the imposition caused onto the addressee (Leech, 2014). This, however, can be suspended in some specific contexts, such as military training (Culpeper, 1996). The topic of politeness and impoliteness will be discussed in detail in the next chapter.

According to Searle (1979: 14), **commissives** commit the speaker to some future course of action. In these cases, the speaker expresses his psychological state of intention, fitting the world to words by himself. Quintessential examples are promises, threats, and refusals:

(5.24) I'll be back. (Said the Terminator T-800 in *The Terminator*)
(5.25) I'll beat you up if you come to her again.
(5.26) I won't consider your plan.

Comparing with Austin's original illustration of commissives, we would find that a number of commissive verbs are excluded, such as *shall*, *intend*, and *favor*, etc. These words do not express the speaker's determination of some future actions. For example, *I favor Hilary Clinton over Donald Trump for the* 2016 *presidential election* does not necessarily mean that the speaker will vote for Hilary. In fact, many people only considered Hilary as "the lesser of two evils" and chose not to vote at all!

The above pagans of commissives may fall into the category of expressives. **Expressives** show the speaker's psychological states of feelings such as pleasures, likes, dislikes, joys or sorrows. See the following examples:

(5.27) I'm sorry for your loss.
(5.28) Congratulations on winning the championship.
(5.29) I'm excited about going to Paris.

It is worth noting that in this category, the speaker does not intend to moderate the world and words in either direction. Instead, the truth of the expressed proposition is presupposed: (5.27) presupposes that the addressee has lost someone precious; (5.28) presupposes that the addressee has won the competition; (5.29) expresses the fact that the speaker has planned to go to Paris. In contrast to its preferred negative meaning in directives, impolite language often functions as intensifiers of the speaker's attitude in expressives, as in (5.30):

(5.30) *The drill sergeant asked the sole purpose of a soldier in the army and Forrest Gump replied that it was to follow the drill sergeant's orders.*
Drill Sergeant: God damn it, Gump! You're a goddamned genius! That's the most outstanding answer I have ever heard! You must have a goddamned I. Q. of 160! You are goddamned gifted, Private Gump!
Forrest Gump (1994)

Finally, **declarations** or **declaratives** are speech acts that change the world via utterances. The successful performance of a declaration ensures that the proposition corresponds to the world. For instance, if the officiator successfully performs the declaration of a marriage, the couples then are legally married; if the U. S. Congress successfully declares war on a country, then the United States is officially at war with that country. Different from the above four types, one may notice that the performing of declaration requires a particular institutional role: Christians won't regard a marriage legal unless the ceremony is performed by a priest; the international bodies won't consider it an official war for America unless the announcement is issued by the U. S. Congress.

These five categories are summarized below (see also in Huang, 2014: 135; Peceei, 1999: 53—54; Yule 1996: 55):

(5.31) Searle's typology of speech acts

Speech act type	Illocutionary point	Direction of fit	Psychological state
Assertives	Commitment of facts	Words to world$_o$	Belief
Directives	Direction of others to do something	World to words	Desire
Commissives	Commitment of actions	Words to world	Intention
Expressives	Expression of feelings	Words to world$_p$	Feel
Declarations	Change of reality	Words change world	Causation

Note: world$_o$ stands for the outside world, and world$_p$ stands for the psychological world.

5.3.3 Direct and indirect speech acts

Before presenting Searle's third advancement of indirect speech acts, we first introduce three basic sentence types: declarative, interrogative, and imperative. Each sentence type typically indicates one type of illocutionary force: a **declarative** is to make a statement, an **interrogative** is to ask a question, and an **imperative** is to command (Lyons, 1977a: 30). A statement is usually associated with asserting, a question questioning, and a directive requesting, as in (5.32)—(5.34) respectively.

(5.32) I want you to open the window. (statement)
(5.33) Can you open the window? (question)
(5.34) Open the window! (command)

In discussing felicity conditions, Searle (1969) observes that the performative verb *promise* can express illocutionary force other than promising. For example,

(5.35) I promise I will kill you if I see you again.

In this case, *promise* no longer commits the speaker to the future act of killing the addressee, but rather serves as a threat to the addressee. This shift of function leads Searle (1975) to identify many more cases where the IFID for one type of illocutionary act is used to perform another type of illocutionary act: the statement of *I want you to fetch some water* is actually a request for water and a simple question *Can you pass me the salt?* is a request for salt. To sum up, a direct speech act is an act with a direct relationship between a structure and a function, and an indirect speech act is the one with an indirect structure-function relation (Yule, 1996: 55).

Indirect speech acts give rise to new questions—how speakers say one thing to mean both that and something else and how hearers manage to figure out the intended meaning of the speaker. Searle (1975: 61) postulates that the successful communication of indirect speech acts relies on the Speech Act Theory, the Cooperative Principle, the factual background shared by the interlocutors, and the hearer's ability to infer; more importantly, an indirect speech act is often associated with convention. Compare the following three sentences:

(5.36) Can you open the window?
(5.37) Do you have the ability to open the window?
(5.38) Are you able to open the window?

Among the above three utterances, only (5.36) is a typical indirect speech act that the hearers could infer a request of opening the window, whereas (5.37) and (5.38), in most cases, confuse the hearers, despite conveying the same semantic meaning.

5.4 Recent developments in Speech Act Theory

In the above two sections, we introduce the two founding fathers' theories of speech acts that are largely formulated in the 1950s to 1970s. The Speech Act Theory has also evolves over the past half a century. Among the many developments, this section briefly introduces three theoretical advancements addressing the study of perlocution, the classification of speech acts, and the sequence of speech acts. These elaborations are by no means exhaustive and serve only as signposts for future research.

5.4.1 Study of perlocution

The first advancement addresses the largely overlooked perlocutionary facet of speech acts. Cohen (1973) first addresses this understudied status of perlocution. He notes that the same perlocution can be directly accomplished by locution, without going through illocution. For example, the parents can urge their children to do their homework by saying that *Finish your homework now* or *Have you done your homework?*.

Campbell (1973) opposes the distinction between illocution and perlocution drawn by Austin and argues that all illocutionary acts surely produce perlocutionary effect and the distinction is simply empty. He also points out that some of the perlocutionary acts described by Austin are simply other complete speech acts. Moreover, Campbell condemns Austin's elimination of poetic and rhetorical languages, defending their essentiality in the meaning-making process.

To remedy the inattention of perlocutionary acts by the linguists, Gaines (1979), in reference to Austin's definition, classifies perlocutionary effects into two main categories: perfected and incipient perlocutionary effects. **Perfected perlocutionary effects** indicate their conceptual completeness, including involuntary (e. g., startle, amuse), voluntary (e. g., insult, entertain), and epistemic subcategories (e. g., confuse, enlighten). In contrast, **incipient perlocutionary effects** have a degree of conceptual incompleteness without the hearer's action. It consists of two subcategories: motivational (e. g., persuade, convince) and practical (e. g., get the hearer to do something). This classification, however insightful, is still flawed on two levels. First, this classification seems to dedicate to perlocutionary acts rather than perlocutionary effects, leaving the unintended cases unaddressed. Second, the incipient category may also manifest a degree of conceptual completeness. For example, if one successfully persuades the other, it already makes a change to the addressee's mind, and the rhetor does not need to adopt further means of persuasion to enforce the act.

Gu (1993) describes the Effect=Act Fallacy to criticize Austin's equating of perlocutionary act to perlocutionary effect. He observes that perlocutionary effects can be unintended, such as the perlocutionary act of alerting someone causes him a heart attack. That is, the actual perlocutionary effects do not merely depend on the speaker, but also on the hearer's recognition of and response to that act.

Dissatisfied with the theoretical discussion of speech acts in the vacuum, Marcu (2000) adopts a data-driven approach to interrogate previous theories of perlocutionary acts with real-world evidence. Among the seven fallacies he listed, we selectively elaborate on two points: First, perlocutionary acts are not consequences of simple locutionary acts. The empirical data suggest that it is very unlikely to consummate the intended perlocutionary effect of someone quits drinking via a simple utterance like *Drinking is bad for your health*. On the contrary, it involves many other explanations, discussions, and in short, many other locutions. Second, speech acts shall not be considered as the basic unit of communication. Admitted by Searle himself (see Section 5. 3. 3), speech act theory is unable to solely explain the multiple perlocutionary effects caused by the same locutionary or illocutionary act. Instead, successful communication requires the employment of a set of persuasive techniques, such as lexical choice (e. g. , eliminating hedges, using metaphors, and replacing abstract terms with specific terms).

From the above elaborations, we can draw two tentative conclusions: First, the treatment of this fussy category of perlocution requires collaborations between pragmaticians and rhetoricians. While pragmatics offers insightful explanations to the inference of meaning (Ariel, 2010), rhetoric provides effective employment of symbols (Herrick, 2013). The marriage between the two subjects is instrumental in explaining how interlocutors interact with each other in the most effective and efficient way. Second, a falsifiable approach to the formulation of pragmatic theories emphasizes the utilitarian nature of scientific studies. The provision of natural data, as notes by Marcu (2000: 1720), is not meant to dismantle theories, but to revise and refine them to best serve the real world. This emerges as a cautionary tale that in the pursuit of academic study, we should always bear in mind the applicability of the theory and prevent our research from deviating from our daily communication.

5.4.2 Classifications of speech acts

Another line of research focuses on the classification of speech acts. While criticizing Austin's original classification for lacking consistent principles, Searle (1975, 1979) complicated his typology with far too many principles: a collection of 12 dimensions and tens of thousands of categories (Sadock 2006). These criteria remain to be open categories, facing the potentials of not covering all types of speech acts. The remainder of this section presents several new attempts of classification.

Ballmer and Brennenstuhl (1981) postulate what they called a lexical approach to speech activity verbs. Based on the core semantic meaning of speech activity verbs, they identify six main semantic centers: expressing emotion, influencing others, verbal struggle, normative behavior, expressing values, and complex discourse functions (ibid: 18). Then, smaller groups are classified according to their semantic meaning and semantic relations with other words. This approach, however, is problematic because it largely relies on the researchers' subjective judgment of semantic meaning.

In discussing speech acts and grammatical structure, Croft (1994), Harnish (1994), and Sadock (1994) come up with three typologies. In Sadock's (ibid) work, he distinguishes three communicative aspects: informational (open for the judgment of truth and falsity), effective (achieving conventional effects), and affective (displaying the speaker's feeling). Harnish (1994) groups his typology via the characteristics of mood in each speech act, i. e. , verbal vs. sentential mood and major mood vs. minor mood. Each mood is subcategorized by linguistic form, illocutionary force, fit compatibility conditions, and inference rules. Moreover, as the leading figure in language typology, Croft (1994) produces a cognitive model of interpersonal interaction to accommodate various speech acts. The two backbones of his theory are the force-dynamic model of interpersonal relations (Talmy, 1988) and the belief-desire-intention model of human behavior (Fauconnier, 1985). The former concerns the action of addition or removal and the latter addresses the speaker's belief, desire, or intention carried out in each speech act.

In the functional camp, Leech (1983: 104) identifies four types of illocutionary functions according to the relationship between the illocutionary goal (the speaker's intention) and the social goal (maintaining comity):

(5.39) Leech's classification of illocution
Competitive: The illocutionary goal competes with the social goal; e. g. , asking, begging, demanding, ordering, etc.
Convivial: The illocutionary goal coincides with the social goal; e. g. , congratulating, greeting, inviting, offering, thanking, etc.
Collaborative: The illocutionary goal is indifferent to the social goal; e. g. , asserting, announcing, instructing, reporting, etc.
Conflictive: The illocutionary goal conflicts with the social goal; e. g. , accusing, cursing, reprimanding, threatening, etc.

Based on Halliday and Matthiessen's (2014) semantic system of speech function, Xiang (2018) proposes a functional classification of speech acts, attempting to use two pairs of binary concepts to cover all the speech acts. On the direction of roles in exchange, a speech act must belong to either giving or demanding; and on the direction of exchanged commodity, a speech act falls into the category of either information or goods & services. Therefore, all speech acts can be classified into four categories: giving information, demanding information, giving goods & services, and demanding goods & services.

Looking through this line of discussion, one might be frustrated with the many theoretical models applied in each classification. While leaving the details of each model aside, we can still easily make two observations on the classification of speech acts: First, we once again witness the application of the Occam's Razor that scholars are trying to reduce the principles towards the best simplest theory possible. Second, in the formulation of different models, we could identify the use of many grammatical, cognitive, social, and psychological theories in pragmatic inquiries. This observation consequently demonstrates the multidisciplinary nature of pragmatics (see Cummings 2005; Green 1996: 1—2).

5.4.3 Sequencing in speech acts

As noted by Taylor and Cameron (1987: 58), the sequencing of an illocutionary act in actual communications is not the main concern of philosophers. Fortunately, this gap is addressed by the Cross-Cultural Speech Acts Realization Patterns (CCSARP) led by Blum-Kulka, House and Kasper (1989). In examining requests and apologies in seven different languages (English, Canadian French, Danish, German, Hebrew and Russian), they observe that a speech act is not realized through a single utterance as Austin (1962) and Searle (1969) suggested, but rather via a sequence of head acts and supportive moves. The head act is the core element of a speech act in Austin and Searle's sense and supportive moves are the linguistic elements added to the head act (e.g., Could you *please* lend me $10?) or associated with the head act (e.g., *I'm running out of cash*. Could you lend me $10?) (see Blum-Kulka & Olshtain, 1984; Blum-Kulka, 1987: 135) Similar results are also found in the aforementioned empirical data in Marcu (2000) and Zhu, Li and Qian (2000).

5.5 Speech acts across cultures and contexts

This section reports the cross-cultural and cross-contextual variations of different speech acts. A detailed study on the rhetorical appeals in Chinese online requests is presented in section 5.6.

5.5.1 Cross-cultural variations

The first thing to bear in mind is that most speech acts are culture-specific and language-specific. For example, a Philippine tribal group called Ilongots uses little speech act of promising in their daily life (Rosaldo, 1982) and the speakers of Yolngu, an Australian aboriginal language, do not seem to perform the speech act of thanking (Harris, 1984). In Chinese culture, the acceptance of the invitation to a dinner party often goes through several rounds of invitation and decline; and an immediate acceptance is considered to be disrespectful to the host (Mao, 1994). Moreover, there is a growing trend that people tend to make insincere promises, such as *I'll see you once I come back* or *I promise this is the last cigarette*! In the remainder of this section, we shall look at some interesting findings in various languages.

One heated discussion is the similarities and discrepancies between the East and the West. In performing requests, Fukushima (1996) surprisingly finds that the Japanese use more direct forms and less supportive moves whereas the British use more supportive moves and conventional forms. Blum-Kulka (1987) observes that Israelis rank *hint* with a lower degree of politeness than British informants do. Byon (2006) elaborates on the unique means of requesting in Korean society (honorifics), challenging the Anglo-American hypothesis of the correlation between indirectness and politeness. After comparing Chinese, American, and Japanese requests, Chen, He, and Hu (2013) cautiously point out that the correlation between West-East geographical progression and indirect-direct cline is too dangerous to conclude. Liu, Deng, and Zhao (2016) analyze how individualism and collectivism influence the Chinese and American political apologies, suggesting that Chinese politicians are more willing to admit their fault and shoulder responsibilities than American politicians.

Moreover, studies also show many variations between English and European languages. For example, Golato (2002) observes far more compliments made by Americans than by Germans; and in responding to these compliments, Germans prefer to make an assessment of them, whereas Americans tend to give appreciation. When apologizing, Russian and Polish speakers are more indirect than their British counterparts (Ogiermann, 2009a). In request, English informants frequently use consultative devices (e. g. , *Can you...*, *Will you ...*), whereas the Germans prefer downtoners (e. g. , *perhaps*, *by any chance*) and Polish and Russian speakers make full use of tense and negation (Ogiermann, 2009b).

In recent years, an increasing number of scholars start to investigate different varieties of major languages such as Turkish-German (Marti, 2006), Cuban Spanish (Ruzickova, 2007), and Dakar French (Johns & Félix-Brasdefer, 2015). Some other researchers tend to inspect areas that are largely ignored. For example, Egner (2006) notes that in some Western African cultures, neither the speaker is bound by his promise nor hearers expect the speaker to fulfill that promise. In Southern Africa, Setswana speakers value the community-based face over the individual face when making apologies (Kasanga & Lwanga-Lumu, 2007). This is particularly significant because their treatment of face incidentally corresponds to that of the Chinese (see Mao, 1994), the civilization that is far away from the African continent. Serving as signposts, these findings are sufficient to demonstrate this burgeoning field of pragmatic inquiry.

5.5.2 Intra-language variations

Within the same language, scholars may also reach different conclusions in their studies of speech acts. For example, Lee-Wong (1994) finds that Chinese requests are more direct than assumed, whereas the data in Chen et al. (2013)

suggest that Chinese are much more indirect than Lee-Wong's conclusion. Similar cases are also found in Japanese: by comparing English and Japanese requests, Fukushima (1996) observes that Japanese tend to use more direct requests because it is considered as an in-group solidarity marker and therefore addresses the requestee's face want of being recognized. Gagné (2010), on the other hand, concludes that the Japanese are more sensitive to requesting, concerning the face threats done upon the requestees. These seemingly contradictory findings are mostly the results of a different composite of research subjects and push scholars to examine speech acts in more specific contexts.

One research trend is to investigate the variation of speech acts across different extra-linguistic factors, such as gender, age, and contextual settings. Holmes (1988: 462 − 463) observes seven differences between New Zealand men and women's performance of compliments. By studying 116 Canadian children, Astington (1988) finds that while adults' conceptualization is closer to Searle's theory, children judge promises based on their outcomes. Context also largely affects the use of speech acts. In cyber communication, interlocutors are inclined to use more conventionalized expressions or add more contextual supports to the performance of speech acts (see Yus, 2011). Xia, Yin, and Lan (2017) investigate how Chinese students respond to compliment in the presence of a third party; Comparing with an earlier study in two parties (Chen, 1993), they find a significant increase in evasion and rejection, indicating the latent influence of the underlying principle of self-denigration in triadic communication. Furthermore, adding interpersonal relationships in the previous three factors, Terkourafi (2001, 2015) proposes a frame-based approach to the study of politeness in Greek requests. Her results show a relatively fixed pattern for formulaic exchanges in different combinations of the above variables.

Another bulk of studies concentrates on the performance of speech acts by non-native speakers from different countries. Kasper and Blum-Kulka's (1993) collection of papers presents five studies of interlanguage speech act performance: thanking, apologizing, complaining, requesting, and correcting. The discrepancies found in their studies between native speakers and learners shed strong pedagogical implications for language teaching. One important section would be the learning of social and cultural conventions of that particular language community (Allami & Naeimi, 2011; Bella, 2012).

Finally, it is important to reiterate that we should not presuppose that different languages definitely display huge differences, whereas the same language or the same culture is always homogenous. For example, although the Chinese and the American often form contrasting communicative patterns, American women share a high degree of similarity with Chinese men and women in terms of egalitarian and hierarchical dimensions (Scollon & Scollon, 1995: 160). The cultural heterogeneity is partly a result of diversified race, religion, and ethnicity, but is also due to its dynamic nature. In a quasi-longitudinal study of Chinese compliment response, Chen and Yang (2010) find an increasing tendency of accepting compliments compared to Chen (1993); they ascribe this change to the increase of western influence across time. To sum up, a scholar would be always aware of and cautious about cultural homogeneity and heterogeneity when researching speech acts.

5.6 Applications: Persuasion in Chinese online forum requests

To better understand how speech acts are delivered effectively, this section, taking Aristotle's three artistic proofs as a critical lens, examines the persuasive strategies employed in Chinese online forum requests. The first section presents Aristotle's rhetorical theorizing of persuasion and the collected data. Sections 5.6.2—5.6.4 illustrate the specific persuasive strategies online users devised along with the directions of ethos, pathos, and logos.

5.6.1 Introduction

Aristotle (2007) takes rhetoric as the ability to find all the available means of persuasion and devises three artistic proofs to account for public forum deliberative: *ethos* concerns projecting self to the audience; *pathos* is about appealing to the audience with emotions; *logos* refers to offering logical reasons to the audience. Since online forum requests are performed in the virtual public sphere, Aristotle's classical theory is suitable for our analysis.

Our data were retrieved from two Chinese online forums: the Q&A section of *Corpus4u*, and the learning section of *Buaabt*[①]. The data were collected according to the following four principles. First, based on Halliday and Matthiessen's (2014) dichotomy between asking for goods-&-services and asking for information, we collected online requests according to requesting action and requesting information. The former includes examples such as asking for academic literature, videos, or syllabuses and the latter contains asking solutions to academic questions. Within each type of request, fifty entries are selected from each of the two forums. Second, to ensure their mastery of netiquette, we chose posters with more than one-year of active online experience. Third, requests involving financial incentives were excluded because the employment of linguistic politeness would be easily suspended in

---

① Corpus4u: http://www.corpus4u.org/forums. Buaabt: http://buaabt.cn/showforum-14.aspx. (2020-5-1)

these cases. Nevertheless, requests with non-financial incentives are retained, such as promising to help back and to share information. Finally, no more than one post will be extracted from the same poster, ensuring the diversity of our sample. Abiding by the above selection criteria, we retrieved a total of 200 instances of online forum requests. In total, we identified eight main strategies under the rubrics of three artistic proofs.

5.6.2 *Ethos*: Projecting self to the requestees

Requesters' character and personality are potentially persuasive to viewers on the forum because they can exhibit the good sense, virtue, and goodwill of the composer (Herrick, 2013). Chinese online requests are mainly carried out by displaying virtue and goodwill.

First, online requests inherit the everlasting theme of deference from Chinese face-to-face communication (Gu, 1990; Ho, 1976: 881), which has been explored in many empirical investigations of Chinese offline communications (Chen, 2015; Hong, 1996; Pan & Kádár, 2011). This strategy is primarily achieved by using politeness markers *qing* and *qiu*. Liu (2000: 13) points out that *qing* is generally translated into English as "please" and is often used as honorifics, indicating the subordination of the speaker compared to the addressee. The verb *qiu*, which literally means "to beg" in Chinese, suggests a larger hierarchal difference between the users. Here are two examples:

(5.40) 请大家推荐几个"转换生成语法""功能语法"论坛或语言学论坛。

《语料库在线》2011.10.05

(5.41) 求各位大神大二物理研究性实验报告作参考。

《北航未来花园》2014.12.08

For example (5.40), by using politeness marker *qing*, the requester puts himself in a lower position compared to the requestee, implying a degree of inferiority. Likewise, the poster in (5.41) conveys his deference to the addressee through the intensified negative politeness marker *qiu*. Compared to the frequent use of *qing* in face-to-face requests (Hong, 1996), *qiu* prevails in online requests. This clear establishment of hierarchy shows that politeness in online communication requires more redressive acts than in face-to-face interaction, indicating that interlocutors express themselves in a more casual, exaggerated, or even dramatic way.

In addition to the massive use of politeness markers, some requesters show deference by stating their inexperience in that matter, as shown in (5.42):

(5.42) 学渣问个问题,关于卫星轨道的……我高中物理学得不好,理论力学也挂过,大学物理也是勉强过的。

《北航未来花园》2015.11.25

The speaker above states that he was underperformed in *Physics* in high school, *Theoretical Mechanics*, and *College Physics*, which are all courses pertinent to physics. Displaying the poor performance of the requestor is a negative politeness strategy because it suggests the relative competence in physics of those potential answerers.

Finally, the expression of deference transcends beyond the linguistic level and could be realized through animated stickers or emojis. These stickers can create a more vivid impression of the inferiority of the requestor. For instance,

(5.43) 我想做一个图片存取数据库,可是小弟不是学这个的呀,对这方面知识欠缺😭,然后网上找了个跟着做,做出来运行的时候是一个空白页啊!😭 有木有学长学弟学姐学妹同级少男少女😁对这个东东熟悉的找时间教育一下小弟好吗😭

《北航未来花园》2015.05.09

The above request perfectly illustrates the use of animated stickers in online forum requests. Four stickers are used in this request to convey deference: the first two stickers animate a person kneeling down and crying out loud, expressing the desperation of not knowing how to build a database and the failure of completing the project based on the online instruction. The third one, depicting a naive figure, highlights the poster's willingness to be catered to. The final sticker of crying reenacts the helplessness of the requestor. While using traditional emoticons such as the smiley face (☺) primarily serves as a positive politeness strategy to build rapport (Kavanagh, 2016; Liu, 2010), animated stickers provide abundant resources to implement negative politeness strategies online.

The second virtue corresponds to *zhi'en* in Chinese culture, which means to acknowledge and appreciate help from others (Huang, 2016: 62). This strategy is realized by explicitly thanking or expressing gratitude to the helpers, as shown in (5.44) and (5.45) respectively:

(5.44) 不知坛子里哪位有 A.P. Cowie 的这本书? 有的话能够发到我邮箱 xxxxx@163.com①。跪谢!

《语料库语言学在线》2014.10.08

---

① Authentic email address is provided in the original request. We replace it with a fake email address for privacy. So do the cell phone number, email address and QQ account provided in the following examples.

(5.45) 有小伙伴想考 9 系的研,可是看完官网发现没有参考书目,哪位学长学姐帮帮忙给一下 609 和 891 的参考书目呀,或者你们学的是哪版的教材。感激不尽!!!

《北航未来花园》2015.04.20

It is also worth noting that these acknowledgments occur before the resolution of the request. This temporal displacement is a result of the asynchronous nature of online communication to which the poster may not respond in time. Therefore, requesters opt to declare that they are indebted to the requestee before the request is addressed, ensuring that the requestee will receive this recognition.

In addition to exhibiting virtues, posters can also build his *ethos* by showing his goodwill or sincerity. Some posters also choose to reveal their identity by attaching personal contact information, such as email address, cellphone number, and social media account. These additional means of contact help requestee respond to the requests more efficiently. Moreover, since online communication is often considered anonymous (Graham & Hardaker, 2017; Yus, 2011), providing personal contact is the first step going on record, showing that the poster is sincere about his request. Here is an example:

(5.46) 求考研专业课力学基础的复习资料,电话联系:12345678901 好心人如有电子版请发 xxxxxx@163.com.

《北航未来花园》2015.05.19

In the above case, the requester posts both his cellphone number and email address as additional means of contact. By revealing his identity online, the poster indicates that his willingness to take responsibility for his post as well as his consideration to provide convenience for the requestee. Consequently, the potential requestee will be more willing to provide the materials to respond to the requester's sincerity. Similar to the expression of virtue, sincerity can also be further exhibited via emoji, as in (5.47):

(5.47) 大二狗晋升下学期,基物实验也跟着来了。可是没有花园学习资料了!!!!!!来发个帖子看看大家谁保存着攻略啊资料啊什么的求共享_(:3)∠)😱😱(楼主 Q12345678)😱😱

《北航未来花园》2015.03.08

5.6.3 *Pathos*: Awakening the emotion of the requestees

Online users frequently implement emotional appeals to alter the viewers' judgment of their relationship, the requester's eagerness, and the urgency of the situation. By applying in-group identity markers, the posters actively identify themselves with the audience. Out of 200 requests, posters manifest

109 instances of in-group identity, which either denote or connotate a sense of community. Since the forums are anonymous, this would establish an immediate close relationship between users and induce them to help. Roughly three-fifths of the 106 entries denote communality or companionship, which are realized through general and specific terms of address. Here are two examples:

(5.48) 大家有没有关于英语关联词、连接词的文章呢？谢谢。

《语料库语言学在线》2012.09.01

(5.49) 同学们有没有认识的外国朋友,需要学习汉语的？搭个伙,我教中文,同时学习英语。

《北航未来花园》2015.05.29

In the first example, the poster addresses viewers as *dajia*, meaning "everyone under certain qualification" in Chinese. In so doing, the requester conveys that he treats all viewers as members of a community, creating an intimate relationship between interlocutors. Other words used in this category include *pengyou* "friend", *xiaohuoban* "buddy", and *tongren* "colleague". This function could also be achieved by using more specific addressing titles that denoting their relations, as is exemplified in (5.49). By addressing the viewers as *tongxue*, "classmates", the speaker claims a more intimate relationship with them, attempting to establish a common identity. This use of specific addressing terms is also found in using *laoshi*, "colleague teachers" in *Corpus4u* that contains a number of teachers and *shixiong/shijie*, "senior academic brother/senior academic sister under the same supervisor" in both forums.

The remaining 46 instances connotate common ground between posters and viewers via cyberspeak. Since everyone in online forums is presumed to be familiar with the use of cyberspeak to imply a membership to the Internet community, which bridges the social distance between requesters and requestees. This function is realized through popular online addressing terms such as *dashen*, "mighty god", *daxia*, "master", and *daxian* "great god", Internet jargon *youmuyou* for *youmeiyou*, "do you have…" and *dongdong* for *dongxi*, "things", and catchphrase such as *liangchen biyou zhongxie* "my name is Liangchen and I will thank you with heavy rewards"[①]. A similar finding is found in Liu (2010). This strategy, however, is invalid if the viewer is unfamiliar with online language or opposes this style of language. For

---

① This catchphrase originates from an online negotiation between two college students over the duty of cleaning a female dormitory. This expression soon went viral on the Internet for its imitation of swordsman language style.

example,

(5.50) 提问:求助大神们有什么免费可用的英汉语料库?
回复:这里的都是老师同学,不是大神。

《语料库语言学在线》2016.11.02

When asking for an English-Chinese corpus, the poster uses a very popular cyberspeak *dashen* to indicate his adeptness of online dialect. This positive politeness strategy, however, is not appreciated by one viewer who comments that there are no mighty gods but only teachers and students in the forum. This communicative failure is not caused by the inexperience of the replier since he is the administrator of the forum nor is due to the unpopularity of *dashen* because it is the single most used addressing term in our data (31 occurrences). In fact, it is most likely to be a result of the commentator's personal judgment of excluding *dashen* as a politeness marker. This example suggests that in-group identity markers may not be upheld by all members of a community and should be used with caution.

The second strategy is to awaken the audience's emotion by strengthening the requester's eagerness to the request. Due to the written-based nature of online forums, the stress of a text is not measured through intonation contour but by exclamation markers or interjections such as *a*, *na*, and *ya*[①]. Here is an example:

(5.51) 跪求 Leech, G (1983). *Principles of Pragmatics*. London: Longman. 电子书,麻烦了!!!!!!!

《语料库语言学在线》2014.11.26

Exclamation marks in the above request intensify the poster's desire to ask for help. Though the viewers do not virtually hear the sound of the speaker, they still could empathize with the requestee's strong desire to obtain an electronic version of Leech's book.

The third strategy is to exaggerate the urgency of the request so as to arouse the sympathy of the audience. This is often achieved by using emphatic adverbs, as is shown in (5.52):

(5.52) 本人正在学习使用 SPSS,好完成论文。发现很多教程都不管用。看了张文彤的书大受启发。但是有些说法可能似懂非懂。自己实在是黔驴技穷了,急于请各位高手们不吝赐教。不胜感激!

《语料库语言学在线》2008.07.05

---

① An alternate explanation of these final particles is that they convey a degree of informality and function as in-group identity marker (Lee-Wong, 1998). In either case, these particles serve as a positive politeness strategy and do not affect the overall prevalence of positive politeness.

Apart from intensifying appreciation through an exclamation mark at the end of the request, example (5.52) also uses emphatic adverbs to elevate strong emotion, including *dou*, "all", *shizai*, "really", and *busheng*, "endless". Since online request does not have a designated addressee, it is highly likely to be overlooked by potential helpers. Other modifiers found in our data include *feichang*, "very", *zhenxin*, "heartfelt", *shifen*, "fully", and *wanfen*, "extremely". With the help of these exaggerations, online requesters could manifest their desperation for help.

While netizens all tend to exaggerate facts to some extent, without an active intensification, the poster's request would be largely overlooked and not be treated seriously. In other words, exaggeration does not merely serve as an enforcement of the request but also appears to be a pertinent feature of online communication. The predilection for exaggeration is furthered by the modifier *gui*, "kneeling down" in Chinese. For instance,

(5.53) 跪求四系叶轮机械原理期末考试资料。

《北航未来花园》2017.01.02

To ask for preparation materials for a test generally will not impose tremendous face damage onto the requestee and sharing these materials with others will not bring life-saving exigency as is suggested by the act of begging in daily conversation. This is a result of the absence of self-politeness in online communication. Chen (2001) notes that, in addition to the face concern for the addressee, the speaker also wants to preserve a certain amount of face. Therefore, a rational speaker will not overly attribute negative values to himself for expressing negative politeness. This constraint, however, is suspended due to the anonymity of online forums. Since the posters construe their own potential face-saving as unnecessary, they are more likely to go to extremes, attributing as many negative values to themselves as possible.

5.6.4 *Logos*: Reasoning with the requestees

The third essential aspect is to provide logical proof to the requestees. Chinese online forum users tend to either explain their reasons for the request in detail or provide a reciprocal condition to persuade the requestees.

First, the poster could opt to convey the reasonableness of his request, implying that the viewers can help the poster out as well as specifying the help (Brown & Levinson, 1987: 128). Our data contain 50 instances of reasoning that emphasize the subjective or the objective aspect of the excuse. We find 28 posts that give subjective reasons concerning the request. These requests either state the requesters' wish or goal or express their failure of solving the problem after personal efforts. Here are two examples:

(5.54) 本人北航四系本科生，今年考研，求北航三系自动控制原理第七章至第九章的课件，望各位大神慷慨相助，谢谢。本人邮箱 29135＊＊12@qq.com。

《北航未来花园》2015.10.25

(5.55) 最近在改一个程序，已经卡了 n 个星期了，不是个事儿啊，主要就是不同文件中的变量放到一个文件中处理，执行过程中不断中断啊，快崩溃了，求大神指教啊，面对面讲讲最好了，天气这么热，我们办公室很凉快。😊救救我吧。

《北航未来花园》2014.05.30

In the first example, the poster explains that his motivation is to be enrolled in the graduate program at his current university. This specification forms cooperation by incorporating requestees into the achievement of the requester's goal and is considered to be a positive politeness strategy. In the second case, by retelling his strenuous efforts spent in rewriting a computer program, the poster demonstrates his inability to debug, justifying his request for help from others. Highlighting the failure of personal effort is a positive politeness strategy because it makes the request reasonable to viewers and waives the impression that the poster wants to gain profits without endeavor. Giving detailed accounts of his past efforts could help identify the mistakes he made and come up with corresponding solutions. Having applied this strategy, the above post is effective in yielding four helpful responses within two days.

While the above sub-strategies elaborate reasons germane to individuals, others justify their requests via providing objective obstacles to their problem-solving. Here is an example：

(5.56) 求助 *Lexicalization and Language Change*，北外论坛上有，但苦于没有账号，而且已经停止注册，有北外论坛账号的能否帮忙下一下。

《语料库语言学在线》2010.09.09

Example(5.56) specifies that the requested material is unavailable because the forum no longer admits new members, indicating that the poster is reasonable enough to turn to those potential viewers with a BFSU forum account. By distancing himself from his request, the requester indicates that the face-threatening act is inevitable and it is not his intention to impose it onto the viewers, providing a stronger reason to ask for help from others.

Another reasoning strategy is to promise something in return for the request. This strategy conforms with a cardinal Principle of Balance in Chinese culture proposed by Gu (1990: 239) that calls for similar behavior in return. For instance：

Chapter 5
Speech Acts

(5.57) 我愿有偿使用,并会在论文中致谢;或者我们也可以合作一起发论文。

《北航未来花园》2017.06.16

The poster promises to pay for the help and to acknowledge the helper's assistance in his paper. He also offers a chance to complete other papers together with the helper. The offer to construct a new research partnership is generous and important to researchers and thus is easy to solicit assistance.

5.7 Review

- **Austin's theory of speech acts**
  - Performatives and constatives
    - Performatives-constatives dichotomy
    - Constatives as a subclass of performatives
  - The performative hypothesis
    - The hidden formula
    - The collapse of performative hypothesis
  - Felicity conditions on performatives
    - Three felicitous conditions
      - Conventional procedure and appropriate person and circumstance
      - Executed by all participants correctly and completely
      - Have requisite thoughts, feelings and intentions, as specified in the procedure, and the relevant parties must do it
    - Two types of infelicities
      - Misfire
      - Abuse
  - Three facets of speech acts
    - Locutionary act
    - Illocutionary act
    - Perlocutionary act
  - Classes of illocutionary force
    - Verdictives
    - Exercitives
    - Commissives
    - Behabitives
    - Expositives
- **Searle's theory of speech acts**
  - Felicity conditions on speech acts
    - Propositional content
    - Preparatory

- Sincerity
- Essential
- Typology of speech acts
  - Governing principles of classification
    - Illocutionary point
    - Direction of fit
    - The expressed psychological states
  - Fivefold categorizations
    - Assertives
    - Directives
    - Commissives
    - Expressives
    - Declarations
  - Direct and indirect speech acts
- **Recent developments**
  - Perlocutionary acts
  - Classification of speech acts
  - The constitution of a speech act
- **Speech act across cultures and contexts**
  - Cross-cultural variations
  - Intra-language variations

Chapter 6

Politeness and Impoliteness

In the Panda Zoo on Liugong Island, Weihai, a sign notes that "I don't like snacks; I don't want to get fat; please don't feed me!", with a cute panda image attached below. From Chapter Five, we get to know that this cute sign carries the same illocutionary force of warning the tourists not to feed the pandas. The seemingly unnecessary personifications of disliking snacks and fearing of getting fat are, in fact, implemented for being polite and creating a rapport environment for the tourists. For the same reason, people usually choose to say *Could you please close the window?*,  instead of blatantly ordering someone by saying *Close the window*! Moreover, apologizing to others clearly reflects a person's level of education because it is conventionally considered as a polite way of reacting. Anyone who has been to Japan is always impressed with or even overwhelmed by the high degree of politeness people show to each other. On a broad level, we have been constantly taught to behave politely by our parents, our teachers, and the society. Politeness is simply "the oil that keeps the interactional hinges from creaking" (Brown, 2017: 383). This chapter focuses on this prevailing phenomenon of politeness and its "evil twin brother" impoliteness in pragmatic studies.

Section 6.1 introduces the basic concepts and classical models in politeness. The burgeoning study of impoliteness is sketched out in Section 6.2. A brief discussion of the future directions of politeness and impoliteness is shown in Section 6.3. Section 6.4 presents an empirical study of politeness in Chinese online forum requests.

6.1 Theorizing politeness

This section first maps out the eight main characteristics of politeness. Then we present three major approaches to politeness, namely, politeness as strategic face management, politeness as a conversational maxim, and politeness as situated evaluation.

6.1.1 Characterizing politeness

Unlike deixis and implicature, politeness is not merely a technical term, but also a word that prevails in our daily communication. Therefore, interlocutors from different cultural backgrounds may hold very different understandings of it. While the Japanese consider politeness as the appropriate allocation of self into the group through conventions (Ide, 1989), the Chinese believe that politeness means respectfulness, modesty, attitudinal warmth, and refinement (Gu, 1990: 239). Its western counterpart, however, is seen as an individualistic concept of face threat avoidance (Brown & Levinson, 1987). In reference to Leech (2014: 4 — 9), this section sketches out eight main characteristics of politeness, pinning down the position politeness research holds in pragmatic inquiries. See the following examples:

(6.1) Fetch me some water!
(6.2) Could you please fetch me some water?
(6.3) If it does not bother you too much, could you please fetch me some water?
(6.4) I beg you for your mercy to fetch me some water.

The first characteristic of politeness is **not obligatory**. A person is not obliged to be polite in communication. For example, one can achieve the same illocutionary act by saying either of the sentences in (6.1) and (6.2) or posting an imperative sign over the cute sign of the Panda Zoo in Weihai. Second, there are **varying gradations** of polite behaviors. Examples (6.1) to (6.4) show an increase in the degree of politeness expressed. However, the exaggerated use of polite language exceeds what is appropriate, as in (6.4), creating a sense of hypocrisy and hence impolite. This also gives rise to the third point that politeness concerns the **sense of what is normal**. When the behavior deviates from what is perceived appropriate in a context, it no longer conveys politeness. Fourth, conveying politeness displays **reciprocal asymmetry** in that it necessarily involves one party giving high value to others or give low value to self. For example, in (6.2) — (6.4), the speaker gives lots of credits to the addressee in exchange for water. The fifth point is that politeness sometimes is **realized through repetition**. A fairly good example is that the Chinese often consider repeated rounds of inviting and declining a meal invitation as polite before finally accepting it (Mao, 1994). Sixth, interactions tend to involve the **transaction of values** between interlocutors. For example, when the speaker asks for water as in (6.2), the addressee usually waivers a portion of value by uttering *No sweat* or *Not a problem*, indicating little burden incurred to the addressee. During this transaction, interlocutors strive to **build an equilibrium of values** between the addresser and the addressee. For instance, after the performance of a drama, the audience usually gives a round of applause to the actors and actresses as a sign of thanking them. In return, the cast will take a curtain call as a polite gesture to balance the transaction of values. When the play is fantastic, the audience may applaud continuously or give standing ovations. In this case, the balance leans towards the audience and the entire cast will take another curtain call to restore the equilibrium. This could go on for several rounds until both the performers and the audience believe that they have even the imbalance. The final point we want to add is that politeness is often a **facilitative action**. By saying words such as *Could you* or *please*, the speaker increases the probability of that action (fetching water) being successfully carried out. Section 5.6 is an illustration of how politeness is strategically employed to achieve communicative goals.

6.1.2 Politeness as strategic face management

The most popular theorizing of politeness is surely Penelope Brown and Stephen Levinson's (1978/1987) seminal work of face redressive strategy. First appeared in essay form in 1978, their work has been put in the spotlight of politeness study; and its reissued book form in 1987 still remains to be the most cited and discussed literature in the realm of politeness research. Based on this version, our introduction will cover positive and negative politeness, the calculation of a face-threatening act (FTA), the face redressive strategy, and criticisms towards their theory.

Borrowing the notion of "face" from Goffman (1967), Brown and Levinson (1987: 62) argue that every interlocutor involves two types of needs for "face", viz. the positive and the negative face. The **negative face** refers to "the want of every 'competent adult member' that his actions be unimpeded by others", whereas the **positive face** is "the want of every member that his wants be desirable to at least some others". People may interact with others via different **face-threatening acts** (FTAs). For example, we usually speak up for someone before asking him or her for a favor. When criticizing someone, we usually use hedges (*I may not be correct* or *I didn't know too much about this*) to make our criticism sound less direct. Consequently, two kinds of politeness emerge: **positive politeness** that addresses interlocutors' positive face and **negative politeness** that preserves the addressee's negative face.

In addition to the concept of "face", Brown and Levinson (1987: 62) also assume that interlocutors are rational that they will choose appropriate linguistic expressions that meet up the payoffs of the FTAs. This requires a way to calculate the weight of an FTA. Brown and Levinson (ibid: 76) propose a formula for its computation:

(6.5) $W_x = D(S,H) + P(H,S) + R_x$

Wx is the weightiness of FTAx the speaker wants to figure out. D stands for the social distance between the speaker and the hearer. For example, a person usually has a much closer social distance with his father than with a stranger. P stands for power from the speaker to the hearer. That is, if the speaker has a higher social status than the hearer, such as a teacher to a student, an employer to an employee, he is able to care less about the consequence of threatening the hearer's face. R stands for the cost-benefit relation in a particular context. In general, to ask for $1 million cash is definitely weighed much heavier than asking for a bottle of water. This relationship, however, will be drastically reversed if the speakers are lost in a desert and desperately looking for water. During the Chinese New Year, neighbors traditionally do not lend anything to others because anything, even dust and trash, symbolizes the incoming fortune of the family and lending stuff means giving away fortune to others. Therefore, to borrow something from the neighbor during the New Year must exert a much higher cost than that of other times.

According to the above calculations of the weightiness of FTAs, Brown and Levinson (1987: 60) propose five super-strategies to account for the various politeness phenomena:

(6.6) Face redressive strategies

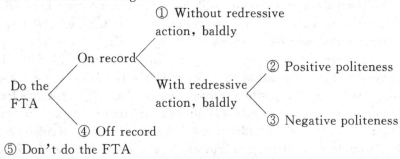

Strategy 1 indicates less concern for the addressee's face and strategy 5 the most concern for the addressee's face damage. Under these five strategies, Brown and Levinson (1987) also postulate a number of output strategies that address the specific aspect of face want. We will illustrate three output strategies under positive, negative politeness, and off record respectively. The first and the fifth are rather self-evident as in doing no redressive action in the former and doing no face-threatening act in the latter.

One typical reflection of positive politeness is to use in-group identity markers such as address forms, in-group language or dialect, jargon or slang, and contraction and ellipsis. Firstly, in order to cater to the addressee's face want of being desirable, the speaker can choose the addressing form that displays a degree of social closeness (e.g., *Lao Wang* "dear Wang", *bro*,

Chapter 6
Politeness and Impoliteness

dude). Secondly, by using in-group language, the speaker is more likely to be recognized as one member of a certain community. One would feel very acquainted with persons speaking the same dialect in a foreign region and more likely to form a close relationship. Similarly, jargon or slang can also establish a degree of solidarity. For example, a teenager may feel more relaxed to talk to someone who uses "233" to mean laugh out loud[①] than using *hehe*. Finally, the use of contraction and ellipsis could manifest a casual style as in the choice of *can't* over *cannot* in spoken English.

Negative politeness is often realized through apologizing. See the following examples:

(6.7) *A salesman tries to promote his products to the customer*:
I know you are very busy, but you would feel refreshed if you try our new product.

(6.8) *Mary runs away from her wedding and Tom says to her*:
I don't want to be judgmental, but you really should think about the consequences.

(6.9) I can think of nobody but you to finish this job.

(6.10) Excuse me, could you close the door?

In (6.7), the salesman redresses the customer's negative face by admitting the impingement of occupying his busy time. Since his negative face is preserved, the addressee is more likely to listen to what the salesman is promoting. In (6.8), Tom indicates his reluctance to be judgmental so that he can offer suggestions to Mary while preserving her negative face. In (6.9), the speaker redresses the addressee's negative face by giving a compelling reason that no other person is competent in doing that job. Moreover, by saying *excuse me*, the speaker in (6.10) begs forgiveness for interruption so as to ask the addressee to close the door.

If both positive and negative strategies are not sufficient to offset the face threat, the speaker usually opts to employ an off-record strategy, such as hints. The speaker does not state his request explicitly but hopes the hearer can work out his request. For example:

(6.11) The room is so stuffy. (Open the window)

(6.12) *A foreigner comes to Beijing and says to his tour guide*:
I heard that Peking Duck is very famous in China. (Take me for Peking Duck)

---

① "233" is the code number for the emoticon "laughing" on a Chinese online forum MOP. Now it is widely used among teenagers to indicate that something is funny. It is often used with multiple "3"s like "23333333".

Based on the theory of indirect speech acts discussed in the last chapter, we can work out that the speaker in (6.11) intends to ask the addressee to open the window. Likewise, the foreigner in (6.12) implicitly asks for Peking Duck by stating that he knows Peking Duck is famous. However, this strategy requires the addressee's ability to infer the implied meaning. Otherwise, for example, the addressee may simply respond that "yes, it is very delicious" and do nothing afterward.

Situated as the most cited literature in politeness research, Brown and Levinson's work also receives heavy criticisms. First, a number of Asian scholars (Gu, 1990; Ide, 1989; Matsumoto, 1989) criticize their theory for being primarily Eurocentric in that it is only suitable to the Western individualism and cannot accommodate the prevailing collectivism in the East. Some others (Mao, 1994; Locher & Watts, 2005) point out that Brown and Levinson's definition of "face" is static and asocial, deviating from Goffman's dynamic and social nature of "face". Moreover, Sifianou (1997) shows that off-record indirectness can convey both positive and negative politeness in Greek, challenging Brown and Levinson's postulation of five super-strategies. Chen (2001) points out that their model only focuses on the face management of others, neglecting the speaker's face want. Furthermore, Leech (2014: 12) argues that their work only considers the redressive side of politeness and fails to address speech acts that voluntarily enhance the hearer's face, such as invitations, compliments, and congratulations. Instead of questioning the validity of face in Brown and Levinson (1987), Jia and Xiang (2018) note that they fail to account for the rationale of employing one output strategy over the other and argue that the choice of different output strategies conforms to an equilibrium of language economy between the speaker's verbal efforts and his communicative utility.

6.1.3 Politeness as a conversational maxim

The concept of "Politeness Principle" first appears in Lakoff's (1973) proposal of pragmatic competence. Its central tenet is to counter Chomsky's claim for universal grammar. Nevertheless, Lakoff's concept has never been fully developed. The systematic advancement of this term was developed by Geoffrey Leech (1980, 1983) and updated in Leech (2007, 2014).

Reviewing the Gricean theory of conversational implicature and Austin's theory of speech acts, Leech (1983) points out that their theories cannot explain why speakers frequently infringe the presumed cooperation and why interlocutors choose indirect speech acts over direct speech acts. To rescue these previous theories, he argues that interlocutors must have observed what he dubbed as **Politeness Principle** in interaction (Leech, 1983: 88). This

Chapter 6
Politeness and Impoliteness

principle is later modified as one super-strategy called the **General Strategy of Politeness**:

> In order to be polite, S expresses or implies meanings that associate a favorable value with what pertains to O or associates an unfavorable value with what pertains to S (S=self, speaker; O=other person(s), especially the addressee).
>
> (Leech, 2014: 90, 221)

Under this overarching constraint, Leech (2007; 2014: 92—98) postulates five pairs of maxims to account for various politeness phenomena[①].

First, the **Generosity Maxim** involves giving a high value to others' wants. It is usually direct as in (6.13) and sometimes even imposing as in (6.14).

(6.13) It is my great honor to work with you.
(6.14) You must come to our house for dinner!

In contrast, the **Tact Maxim** requires the speaker to associate a low value to his own wants. The related speech acts are generally indirect, usually with hedges involved (hedges are italicized in the following two examples).

(6.15) Do you, *by any chance*, have five dollars? (Lend me five dollars)
(6.16) *If it does not bother you so much*, could you please close the door?

The second pair addresses the attribution of qualities to the speaker and the others. The **Maxim of Approbation** is about giving a high value to others' qualities, such as making compliments, as in (6.17). In some cases, the speaker may compliment the addressee beyond his ability, as in (6.18).

(6.17) You are such a wonderful person.
(6.18) (To an English learner) You speak like an American.

And the **Maxim of Modesty** describes speakers' predilection to give a low value to their own qualities. This often applies to the responses of compliments, as in (6.19) and (6.20).

(6.19) You are flattering me. I'm not that good.
(6.20) My success largely relies on the support of my school and my team.

The third pair concerns the obligation between the speaker and the others. The first part requires the speaker to allocate a high value to his obligation to others

---

① In his earlier theory, Leech (1983: 132) proposed six maxims: Tact, Generosity, Approbation, Modesty, Agreement, and Sympathy Maxims. The extended version is more systematic in that it is all constrained by the same overarching principle, i. e., General Strategy of Politeness.

and the second part is about lowering the value imposed on others. **The Maxim of Obligation of S to O** is illustrated in (6.21) and (6.22); and the **Maxim of Obligation of O to S** is shown in (6.23) and (6.24).

    (6.21) I am so sorry about these inconveniences.
    (6.22) I am deeply indebted to your help.
    (6.23) (In responding to someone's thanking) No sweat.
    (6.24) It's a piece of cake.

In the fourth pair, **Agreement Maxim** is to give a high value to O's opinions. The speaker expresses his approval of the addressee's opinion, as in (6.25). Leech (2014: 97) suggests that English speakers tend to agree with their opponents before giving rebuttals, as in (6.26).

    (6.25) **Xiaowang**: I think Gaokao is a terrible policy.
            Xiaoli: I couldn't agree with you more.
    (6.26) **Xiaowang**: I think Gaokao is a terrible policy.
            Xiaosun: I agree with you. But it is the fairest way we have so far.

On the speaker's side, **Opinion-reticence Maxim** constrains the speaker to associate a low value to his own opinions. Lots of hedges and parentheticals are used under this maxim. For instance,

    (6.27) *As far as I am concerned*, this is the best solution.
    (6.28) The result, *I guess*, would not be promising.

The final pair deals with the interlocutor's feelings. **Sympathy Maxim** associates a high value to O's feelings. This is commonly used to express sympathy or empathy towards the addressees.

    (6.29) I'm sorry to hear that your father just passed away.
    (6.30) I am so happy about your success.

In contrast, the Feeling-reticence Maxim requires the speaker to give a low value on his own feelings. Following this maxim, the speaker tends to express his feelings indirectly.

    (6.31) **Tony**: How are you these days.
            Sarah: It's OK…

Finally, Leech (2014: 98) notes that the maxims that preserve the others' values usually have stronger power than those qualifying the speakers' values. The maxims that are listed in the front (e.g., Generosity and Tact Maxims) seem to enjoy higher priorities than those listed in the back (e.g., Sympathy and Feeling-reticence Maxims).

In addition, Leech (1983, 2014) also proposes two minor principles to account for the occasions where the Politeness Principle is violated. **Irony Principle** describes the act that is superficially being polite, but actually impolite. It is often observed in exaggeration or understatement (Leech, 1983: 143). For example,

(6.32) *John spent seven minutes on his 1000-meter physical test:*
Tom: John, you are as fast as light.
(6.33) *John is good at handcrafts.*
Tom: Doing handcrafts is all he is good at.

In (6.32), John's physical test score is rather low in that the passing score is four and a half minutes. One could work out Tom's irony if he observes this degree of exaggeration. In (6.33), John may be good at a variety of things, such as academic studying or cooking. Tom's comment, however, understates John's ability, confining his strongpoints to handcrafts. This is also considered as an irony.

In contrast to the Irony Principle, the **Banter Principle** describes "an offensive way of being friendly" (Leech, 1983: 144). It is observed when the speaker says something obviously untrue or impolite. For example,

(6.34) *A friend of Usain Bolt says to him:*
Bolt, you run like a turtle.
(6.35) *John meets his old friend Tom and says:*
You bastard, how come you didn't reach me in 20 years?

In (6.34), it is obviously untrue to say that Bolt runs slowly because he is the Olympic champion of sprint and is possibly the fastest person on earth. Therefore, his friend's comment is more likely to be construed as banter. Similarly, the impolite vocative "you bastard" is often inferred as a way of expressing solidarity between two friends.

To sum up, different from Brown and Levinson's anthropological view, Leech views politeness as a part of conversational implicature that is jointly governed by the Cooperative Principle, the Politeness Principle, the Irony Principle, and the Banter Principle.

Leech's theory is also engaged by a number of scholars. Thomas (1995: 168) questions the applicability of these maxims. She finds that some of these constraints may be universal, whereas others are culture-specific. A similar problem is also identified in Gu's (1990) modification of Tact and Generosity Maxims. Moreover, Chen's (2001) criticism of Brown and Levinson is also applicable to Leech's conversational maxims. Finally, Brown and Levinson (1987: 4) reject the necessity of a principle of politeness, arguing that politeness is easy to be undermined and should not be abstracted as a principle. Following them, Huang (2007: 37) contends that Leech's expansionist approach goes against the spirit of Occam's Razor. Leech (2014) responds that the premise of expansion is to address the insufficient explanatory power of the Cooperative Principle. This meets up the corollary of Occam's Razor that entities can proliferate with necessity. Moreover, the Politeness Principle could also be treated as a maxim under the Cooperative Principle rather than regarded as a separate principle. This classification rectifies its relationship with the Cooperative Principle, catering to its less robustness as an independent principle, but also addresses its importance in human communication.

6.1.4 Politeness as situated evaluation

After the celebration of the New Millennium, politeness studies underwent a postmodern turn which is defined as a "theoretical move which questions all concepts and evaluations and is sceptical of all attempts at grand narrative or metanarrative that is, all overarching theories which attempt to generalise or universalise" (Mills, 2011: 28). This school of inquiry is represented by Arundale (2006, 2010, 2013), Eelen (2001), Locher (2004, 2006), Locher and Watts (2005), Mills (2003), and Watts (1992, 2003). Based on the cross-cultural counterexamples raised by the Asian scholars (e.g., Blum-Kulka, 1987; Ide, 1989; Mao, 1994; Matsumoto, 1989), Watts (2003: 23) contends that a theory of politeness should never be predictive or universal. Following Watts (1992), Eelen (2001) criticizes that the study of politeness should be conducted solely under the layman's understanding (**first-order politeness**) rather than under the scientific conceptualization of politeness (**second-order politeness**). All these objections push scholars to develop theories that are situated and not overgeneralized.

The main thrust of the early attempts is developed by Locher and Watts (2005), which is a follow-up of Watts (2003). Their model of **Relational Work** is constructed on the basis of first-order politeness and a discursive bottom-up methodology. Based on Bourdieu's (1990) notion of *habitus* (predispositions of an act), Locher and Watts (2005) argue that most of the instances incorporated in Brown and Levinson's and Leech's conceptions of "politeness" are socially appropriate "politic behavior" and do not manifest politeness *in toto*. Therefore, the discursive disputes over "rude" "impolite" "politic" "polite" and "over-polite" should all be worked out by carefully examining individuals' judgments on that particular act (van der Bom & Mills, 2015).

This approach, on the one hand, provides a successful critique to the traditional politeness theories; but on the other hand, this *a priori* rejection to the possibility of prediction also rejects the possibility of theorizing politeness at any level and offers nothing even on a descriptive level (Terkourafi, 2005: 245-246), rendering analyst to be "redundant" in politeness research

(Holmes, 2005: 115). Moreover, Haugh (2007) contends that it is unpractical to disassociate analysts from participants because the researchers cannot directly attain the participants' conceptualization of politeness and have to rely on an educated guess. In other words, although advocating a pure basis of first-order politeness, relational work inevitably pins down its study by introducing a second-order definition of first-order politeness (Terkourafi, 2005: 243). More importantly, the demarcation between "polite" and "politic" renders the theory to be explanatively inadequate to account for the production of speech acts, i. e. , the sole reliance on *post hoc* evaluation is not applicable to analyzing the speaker's choice of communicative strategies.

The recent development in the postmodern trend tends to emphasize the dynamic reciprocity between and among interlocutors (Arundale, 2006, 2010, 2013; Grainger, 2011; Haugh, 2007; O'Driscoll, 2007). One notable advancement is Arundale's (2006, 2010, 2013) **Face Constituting Theory** (FCT). Construing "face" as interactionally achieved, FCT takes dyad rather than individual as the basic unit of analysis, addressing how face is jointly constructed through mutual constraints of both the speaker and the hearer (Arundale, 2010). Its major contribution is that it provides a rather interactive conceptualization of face and consequently reduces the potential interference of analysts in the interpretation of politeness. The over-reliance on the dynamic interactiveness, however, renders the theory to be inadequate to account for asynchronous messages, such as e-mail and online forum discussion or unilateral communications where the addressee is not required or unable to respond, e. g. , in public announcements, radio broadcasts, and television entertaining programs.

To recap the postmodern school of politeness, we find that this line of theorizing offers critical rebuttals towards Brown and Levinson (1987) and Leech (1983, 2014), pointing out the discrepancies existing between a scholarly interpretation of a certain speech act and that of a common conception. Consequently, the postmodern models of politeness emphasize on the situatedness of communicative encounters, rejecting any *a priori* presumptions of politeness held by the interlocutors. This approach, nevertheless, requires further reconsideration on the following three points. First, while primarily focusing on the interpretation end of politeness for a certain speech event, postmodern theories fail to cater to its production end, incapable of expounding how a speaker generates politeness speech acts at first hand. Second, the heavy dependence on the immediate context hinders its application in cases where the supporting context is unavailable, such as non-face-to-face interactions (e. g. , telephone calls), asynchronous communications (online forum discussions), or indirect participation (public announcements).

Finally, the theory has few practical or pedagogical implications for interlanguage or cross-cultural communications. Their strong rejections of the predictive nature of politeness render their theories to be too vague to produce any hands-on politeness formulae for language learners.

6.2 Theorizing impoliteness

Although studies of face attack or aggravating languages can be traced back to Goffman (1967), Lachenicht (1980) and Austin (1990), impoliteness phenomena are generally considered as marginal occurrences of urgency or efficiency (Brown & Levinson, 1987: 62) or as what children learn to avoid (Leech, 1983: 105). However, Culpeper (1996) finds that impoliteness is prevalent in the case of military training. Impoliteness behaviors are often taken as an effective measure to shape the soldiers' physical and psychological fitness. Moreover, Dynel (2015) identifies 12 major types of impoliteness discourse: military training, legal discourse, classroom discourse, talk in the workplace, institutional discourse, YouTube interactions, Internet forums, political broadcast, exploitative quiz and talent shows, films and drama, exploitative reality shows, and literature. These findings suggest that impoliteness phenomena are important in our daily communication and need to be theorized.

Following Culpeper (2011: 23) and Dynel (2015), we take "impoliteness" as an umbrella term to cover all types of intentional face-attacks (see Terkourafi, 2008 for her justification of "rudeness" over "impoliteness"). In the remainder of this section, we introduce three major types of impoliteness behaviors and three branches of impoliteness modeling.

6.2.1 Types of impoliteness

Based on the functions displayed in interaction, impoliteness can be classified into affective, coercive, and entertaining impoliteness (Culpeper, 2011: 221)[①]. First, **affective impoliteness** refers to the speaker's emotional display via impolite language. Common examples are *goddamn*, *fucking*, *hell*, *holy shit*, etc. Second, **coercive impoliteness** is the exercise of power to enforce a realignment of values between the speaker and the hearer. It is worth noting that although being coercive, the enforced actions are mostly legitimate, such as the police officer interrogating a suspect. Finally, **entertaining impoliteness** produces pleasure for someone by being impolite to the other. Du

---

① Kasper (1990) terms these three categories as **rudeness lack of affect control**, **strategic rudeness**, and **ironic rudeness** respectively.

(2005: 248—249) observes that African Americans tend to play a language game called "playing the dozens": interlocutors tease each other's family members in terms of their personality and physical appearance, as shown in (6.36) and (6.37).

 (6.36) Your mother is so dumb; she couldn't pass a blood test.
 (6.37) Your mother is so old; she knew Burger King when he was just a prince.

One may notice that these impolite expressions are highly creative. In contrast, linguistic politeness often falls into the expectation of the interlocutors (Terkourafi, 2015) or abides by social norms (Fraser, 1990; Meier, 1995, but see Watts, 2003 for a different view).

In addition, the above three functions can be fulfilled by one utterance. For example, in Quentin Tarantino's celebrated movie *Pulp Fiction*, Jules is trying to stop Vincent from shooting one of the robbers:

 (6.38) Jules: You ain't gonna do a goddamn thing, now hang back and shut the fuck up.

Pulp Fiction (1994)

By using profanity (*goddamn*), Jules displays his strong anger towards Vincent for attempting to kill the robber, achieving the function of affective impoliteness. In the meantime, the impolite imperative in the second half of the sentence enforces the action, coercing Vincent to step back and stop talking. In this life-or-death moment, impolite coercion is far more instrumental than a polite request. For the moviegoers, to watch this impoliteness gives rise to a sense of emotional pleasure. In fact, the whopping 265 instances of *fuck* in the entire movie is one of the highlights that attracts and entertains the audience.

6.2.2 Impoliteness as strategic face attacks

Measuring against the three major treatments of politeness, we introduce three corresponding approaches to impoliteness. The first one views impoliteness as strategic face attacks. In reference to Brown and Levinson's (1987) five super-strategies of face supporting, Culpeper (1996: 356) postulates five counterstrategies of face attacking, as shown in (6.39).

 (6.39) Impoliteness strategies

  1. **Bald on record impoliteness**: the FTA is performed in a direct and concise manner in cases where face is relevant. E.g., cursing someone in public.

  2. **Positive impoliteness**: strategies used to damage the addressee's positive face want. E.g., being disinterested in others, excluding

others from the group, and ignoring others.

3. **Negative impoliteness**: strategies used to damage the addressee's negative face want. E. g. , using taboo words, stepping into others' private space, and nudging others to be impolite.

4. **Sarcasm** or **mock politeness**: the FTA that is performed via insincere politeness. E. g. , complimenting someone against facts.

5. **Withhold politeness**: the absence of necessary politeness. E. g. , not thanking someone after receiving his help.

It is worth noting that impoliteness is commonly manifested by multiple strategies (Culpeper, Bousfield & Wichmann, 2003; Lachenicht, 1980). For example,

(6.40) Get the fuck out of our community.

According to the above five strategies, one can easily observe that (6. 40) employs both positive impoliteness strategy (excluding others from the group by forcing someone to leave) and negative impoliteness strategy (using taboo word *fuck*).

These five strategies are updated in Culpeper (2005) by incorporating Spencer-Oatey's (2002) renewed interpretation of face. Bousfield (2008) collapses Culpeper's five super-strategies into on record and off record strategies. In addition, Culpeper, Bousfield and Wichmann (2003) also emphasize the contribution of prosody in impoliteness interpretation. It is important to bear in mind that these impoliteness strategies do not guarantee impolite interpretation, and the interpretation of impoliteness relies heavily on contexts (Culpeper, 2010). For example, imperatives are usually considered impolite due to its directness. However, in military combat, ordering your fellow combaters to take cover is the most salient way of showing considerateness.

6.2.3 Impoliteness as conversational maxims

In reference to Culpeper's (2005) definition of impoliteness, Leech (2014) argues that a theory of politeness is generally applicable to a theory of impoliteness. Based on his General Strategy of Politeness (see Section 6.2.2), Leech (2014: 221) postulates General Strategy of Impoliteness: "In pursuing the goal of impoliteness, S will express/imply evaluative meanings that are favorable to S and unfavorable to O"; and the correspondent maxims are listed as follows:

Chapter 6
Politeness and Impoliteness

(6.41)

Maxim violated	Typical speech types	Examples
Generosity	Refusing, threatening	I don't want your stuff.
Tact	Ordering, demanding	Give that to me!
Approbation	Insulting, complaining, telling off	He is the one who broke the window.
Modesty	Boasting, being complacent	I'm the best in the business.
Obligation to O	Withholding thanks or apologies	-Here you are. -(silent)
Obligation to S	Demanding thanks and apologies	You didn't say *thank you*.
Agreement	Disagreeing, contradicting	That's nonsense!
Opinion reticence	Being opinionated	You have to listen to me!
Sympathy	Expressing antipathy to O	How could you do that to her?
Feeling reticence	Grumbling, grousing	Everything is going horribly wrong!

In addition to the realizations governed by the above ten maxims, impoliteness is also expressed via taboo languages, such as profanity (e.g., *Jesus*, *God damn it*) and swearing (e.g., *fucking*, *motherfucker*). The use of taboo language is often considered as direct impoliteness and is hard to redress by politeness devices. For example,

(6.42) Would you mind taking away your fucking feet?

Swearing in the above case can be hardly modified into a polite expression even if the negative politeness strategy of question is employed[①].

In contrast to the above blatant use, impoliteness can be achieved implicitly through irony. It requires the hearers to work out impoliteness that is implied by the speaker. One advantage is that the speaker can take this indirectness as a defensive strategy: the speaker can cancel the potential impoliteness implicature and prevent it from escalating to a violent conflict

---

① A recent study (Murphy, 2019) shows that a decent number of British native speakers consider non-canonical apologies such as *I'm sorry you are such an arsehole* as appropriate apologies. This suggests that the mismatching of polite and impolite expressions should be further investigated in contexts.

(Leech, 2014: 224), as in (6.43).

 (6.43) *Tom lost John's iPad.*
   John: Tom, you are a meticulous person.
   Tom: Don't do that. I said I'm sorry.
   John: No, no, no. I don't mean that. I mean you are always careful and you can definitely recall where you put it.
   Tom: Okay, I'll try.

In the above case, John appears to be ironic which makes Tom even guiltier. This implicature is soon canceled when John further explained that he thought Tom is a meticulous person and would not really lose it. Therefore, the same utterance is modified from irony to encouragement.

6.2.4 Impoliteness as a discursive practice

In general, discursive scholars tend to treat impoliteness along with their theorizing of politeness (Locher & Watts, 2005; Arundale, 2006). They attempt to come up with one unified theory to accommodate both politeness and impoliteness phenomena. As illustrated in Section 6.2.3, these scholars tend to take impoliteness as the opposite side of politeness on the spectrum of interpersonal relationships. These diversified models display two general features of contextual sensitivity and interactive construction.

First, the discursive scholars believe in the determinate power of context in a theory of impoliteness. Therefore, they argue that impoliteness is not inherent in linguistic forms, but is evaluated by the hearer according to social conventions (Eelen, 2001; Mills, 2005; Watts, 2003). This contextual sensitivity gives rise to the second feature that impoliteness is jointly constructed by the speaker and the hearer. That is, what matters is not the speaker's utterance but the **judgment** made by the hearers and the speaker's response to that of the hearers. Furthermore, Juanchich, Sirota, and Bonnefon (2019) show that individuals' judgment of politeness is not determined by the linguistic expressions *per se*, but by interlocutors' willingness to engage in that particular act. Their findings show that when people are unwilling to donate to a charity, they tend to rate the donation request as less polite, maintaining their higher moral ground of "I would donate if you could have asked politely".

6.3 Some potential issues in (im)politeness research

Although so much has been done, politeness and impoliteness research still contains a number of contentions and research potentials. First, should politeness and impoliteness be researched under the same theoretical model or should they be theorized in their own merits? On the one hand, impoliteness is traditionally considered as the "dark side" of politeness (Austin, 1990) and should be treated together; on the other hand, it is also treated as an effective means of communication that works with a different mechanism compared to that of politeness (Mills, 2005). In recent years, the rise of interpersonal pragmatics offers a new perspective to put politeness and impoliteness into a broader interpersonal continuum (Locher, 2015; Ran, 2018; Locher & Graham, 2010; Ran & Liu, 2015).

Second, to what degree can we theorize politeness and impoliteness phenomena? While it is commonly agreed among scholars that politeness and impoliteness do not reside in linguistic forms (Watts, 2003; Mills, 2005; Locher & Watts, 2005), it is also widely recognized that certain linguistic expressions conventionally signal politeness and impoliteness (Culpeper, 2010; Leech, 2014; Terkourafi, 2015). As pointed out in Brown (2017), the current studies focus more on the empirical research of cultural diversities but overlook cross-cultural parallels. The more urgent task is to determine the degrees of generalities we can extract from their linguistic realizations and the degrees of contextual viabilities we permit. Moreover, the rise of the postmodernist approach pushes scholars to interrogate the evaluation of (im)politeness and the factors that influence the evaluators (in most cases, the conversation participants) (Davies, 2018; Haugh, 2018).

Third, while politeness and impoliteness have been majorly examined from the direction of solidarity, power has been largely ignored or understated (see a few attempts in Culpeper, 2008; Shibamoto-Smith, 2011; Holmes & Stubbe, 2014). In many cases, instead of creating a rapport, the primary focus of interlocutors is to enforce actions through the exercise of power. Moreover, it is rather untenable to use a few politeness formulae to successfully regulate interpersonal relationships. Instead, the management of sincere rapport is an accumulative process that requires long-time socialization, involving both linguistic behaviors and non-linguistic attributes, such as personalities and levels of education. In contrast, power relations is much more salient. Interpersonal relations can be immediately enhanced, maintained, or degraded through the exercise of power. A theory centered on power could offer insights to unified explanations of politeness and impoliteness.

In addition to these theoretical contentions, scholars also attempt to address the research gaps that are generated out of updated technologies and new lifestyles. One prominent technological breakthrough is the emergence of the Internet that prospers computer-mediated communication, such as online forums, WeChat, and WhatsApp. The asynchronicity of online responses between the interlocutors, the shortage of relevant contexts, and the anonymity of interlocutors consequently breed brand new treatments of politeness and impoliteness (see Graham, 2007; Hardaker, 2010; Dynel, 2012). The following section will provide a brief analysis of how politeness is displayed in Chinese online forum requests.

Another development is the investigation germane to entertaining impoliteness. In recent years, the entertainment business constitutes a huge portion of our daily lives, including *Saturday Night Live*, *The Daily Show*, *The Colbert Report* and many other television programs. The study of humorous or expletive languages is the one that grows out of these entertaining programs (Culpeper, 2005; Dynel, 2013; Gordon, 2013). This branch of research demonstrates the prevalence of impoliteness phenomena in everyday interactions, justifying the communicative salience of impolite languages.

In short, combining the trending postmodernism and pragmatism, (im)politeness scholars are striving to construct models that are general enough to explain a range of (im)politeness phenomena and, in the meantime, local enough to ensure that these behaviors are virtually accounted for. To achieve this goal, researchers are expected to interrogate (im)politeness in language socialization, learning and teaching, historical, gender, regional, intercultural, and cross-cultural variations and examine these changes framed in contexts such as workplace, service encounters, health settings, legal settings, political exchanges, fictional texts, and digital communication (Culpeper, Haugh & Kádár, 2017).

6.4 Applications: Politeness in online forum requests

Applying Brown and Levinson's (1987) model of politeness, this section explores the relatively underdeveloped study of politeness strategies in Chinese online forum requests, examining the differences and similarities between requests in cyberspace and the physical world. Section 6.4.1 introduces the research design and data collection. Sections 6.4.2—6.4.4 present the employment of bald on record, positive, and negative politeness strategies respectively.

6.4.1 Introduction

We adopt Brown & Levinson's (1987) face redressive model in our study of Chinese online requests. As shown in section 6.2.1, Brown and Levinson's model involves five super-strategies of politeness: bald on record, positive politeness, negative politeness, off record, and withhold politeness. Following Maricic (2001), the last two strategies are excluded because of their scarcity and the difficulty of hinting in a text-based online forum.

Chapter 6
Politeness and Impoliteness

Our data are extracted from *douban*, a Chinese-based online forum popular among college students. The high level of education can partially ensure that the viewers have a good sense of social etiquette for requesting, i.e., the speakers have at least enough knowledge of how to behave properly in daily settings. We conveniently selected 40 instances of online requests on this forum. The selection process met the following two criteria: first, each collected instance must have at least five responses, serving as a *post hoc* evaluation of its effectiveness. Second, questions for pure information are excluded, such as asking for the timetable of the train. This is to ensure that there was an actual imposition on the potential addressee and therefore needed to invoke politeness strategies.

6.4.2 Bald on record strategies

First, bald on record strategies are found both in cases of non-minimization of the face threat and cases of FTA-oriented bald on record usage. The table below features the distribution of linguistic realizations of bald on record strategies:

(6.44) Bald on record strategies in the data

Bald on Record	Linguistic realizations	Examples
Overriding face concern	Imperatives	求助！
	Direct questions	有没有人帮忙解答下？
	Assertive request	有关网络负面口碑的问卷
Addressing face concern	Imperatives	留下你的链接,定回填！

Among the 40 instances of online requests, we find 28 out of 40 are used to override face concern and 12 instances for addressing face concern. This predominant use of bald on record strategy can be largely ascribed to the textual nature of the request. In other words, the polite concern is subordinated to the concern of clarity. And the requestees' face wants are satisfied via positive politeness strategies. In addition, the 12 instances of imperative in the bottom column indicate that bald on record strategies could be considered as offers in the form of a request. By asking the requestees to leave the link of other surveys, the speaker offers an open promise as a reciprocal help and therefore reduces the imposition that falls upon the requesters. Nevertheless, this reduction only comes into effect when the requestee is also seeking for help.

6.4.3 Positive politeness strategies

Second, positive politeness strategies address the requestees' need for social approval. This is achieved by claiming the common ground, conveying that S and H are cooperators, and fulfilling H's want for something in exchange (Brown & Levinson, 1987: 101—129).

(6.45) Positive politeness strategies in the data

Positive politeness	Linguistic realizations	Examples
Claim common ground	Using overstatement	万能的豆友
	Attending to the requestee	亲们
	Expressing gratitude	非常感谢！
	Using emojis and signs	'~~~' '(｡•́︿•̀｡)' '!!!'
	Address forms	大佬；大神；豆友
	Using in-group language or dialect	求助 B 组各位大神
	Using humorous language	江湖救急
Convey that S and H are cooperators	Asserting S's knowledge of H's concern	绝对安全
	Asserting reciprocity	绝对回填
Fulfill H's want for some X	Asserting material reward	求带东西，可以接机
	Asserting psychological reward	好人一生平安！

In this category, we identified 102 linguistic realizations of positive politeness strategies in 40 instances of online requests. This clearly shows the multiplicity in the application of politeness strategies in online forum requests. This abundant use can be considered as a major compensation to the face damage created in expressing requests directly.

Moreover, the prevalent use of exaggerated expressions, such as *dashen*, *wannengde*, and *guixie* shows that when the addressees' identities are unspecified, the speaker tends to maximize the benefits towards the addressees. This tendency coincides with Leech's (1983) Politeness Principle that the speaker tends to add as many positive values as possible to the hearers. The anonymity of this online forum renders that speakers require little necessity to preserve their individual face want, contrasting to Fraser's (1990) and Chen's (2001) objection to Leech's maximization of positive attributes. Moreover, the repeated use of exclamation markers reinforces the sincerity of the speakers, compensating for the concern of insecurity generated induced by the anonymous nature of the Internet.

6.4.4 Negative politeness strategies

In addition to actively enhancing the requestees' face, requesters also opt to address their negative face wants. This is commonly realized through giving freedom of action, minimizing threat and minimizing imposition (Maricic, 2001: 413). The uses of these strategies are shown in (6.46).

(6.46) Negative politeness strategies in the data

Chapter 6
Politeness and Impoliteness

Negative politeness	Linguistic realizations	Examples
Give freedom of action	Using questions and modal verbs	能帮我找本书拍给我么?
Minimizing threat	Using politeness formulae	恳请大家帮帮忙。
	Asserting minimal	问卷也不涉及私人信息。
	Showing deference/vulnerability	毕业狗;我真是个大傻子
Minimizing imposition	Asserting apologies	不好意思,请耽误大家两分钟帮我填个问卷。
	Asserting minimal effort	题不多,一分钟搞定。
	Providing conditional options	大家有空帮忙填下问卷哈。

The use of politeness formulae occupies roughly two-thirds of the 63 realizations of negative politeness. This mirrors the distribution of politeness strategies in face-to-face communications (see Marti, 2006; Kim & Farashaiya, 2012), indicating that conventionalized politeness formulae are applicable in online contexts.

Furthermore, we also identify a unique use of negative politeness strategy when expressing deference and vulnerability. Similar to the aforementioned exaggeration in positive politeness, requesters do not need to meet up the constraints of self-politeness shown in Chen (2001). Consequently, some web users will opt to further denigrate themselves, such as using animal metaphors (*biyegou* "senioritis"). While implicating the sense of humbleness of the speakers, these denigrations could also convey a degree of incivility for those who are not familiar with these expressions.

6.5 Review

- **Theorizing politeness**
    - Eight characteristics of politeness
        - Not obligatory
        - Varying gradations
        - Sense of what is normal
        - Reciprocal Asymmetry
        - Realized through repetition
        - Transaction of values
        - Build an equilibrium of values
        - Facilitate actions
    - Politeness as face management (Brown & Levinson)
        - Positive and negative politeness
        - Calculation of FTA
        - Face redressive strategy

- Bald on record
- Positive politeness
- Negative politeness
- Off record
- Do not do FTAs

○ Politeness as conversational maxim (Leech)
- The General Strategy of Politeness (Politeness Principle)
  - Generosity
  - Tact
  - Approbation
  - Modesty
  - Obligation of S to O
  - Obligation of O to S
  - Agreement
  - Opinion-reticence
  - Sympathy
  - Feeling-reticence
- Irony Principle
- Banter Principle

○ Politeness as situated evaluation (Postmodernist scholars)
- Early attempts
  - E. g. Relational work
- Later developments
  - E. g. Face Constituting Theory

• **Theorizing impoliteness**
  ○ Types of impoliteness
  - Affective
  - Coercive
  - Entertaining
  ○ Impoliteness models
  - Impoliteness as strategic face attacks
  - Impoliteness as conversational maxims
  - Impoliteness as discursive practices

Chapter 7

Research Methods

In the previous chapters, we went through five essential topics in pragmatic inquiry: deixis, presupposition, implicature, speech act, and (im)politeness. Having learned these theoretical concepts, one may still wonder how to put these abstract notions in practice. In this chapter, we will focus on the commonly used research methods in pragmatics. Nunan (1992: 3) notes that academic inquires include a question, a problem, a hypothesis, data, and the analysis and interpretation of data. To help beginners start their own research and develop a research paper, Section 7.1 directs emerging scholars to identify potential research questions; Section 7.2 introduces methods to harvest convincing data for analysis; and the specific analytical methods are illustrated in Section 7.3.

7.1 Literature mining

This section first maps out four types of research questions we could raise and then introduces three ways to unearth relevant literature: review articles and bibliographies, search engine and database, and bibliometric analysis and knowledge visualization.

7.1.1 Four types of exigences

The composition of a research article requires scholars to identify a problem in the current research paradigm. This type of "imperfection marked by urgency" is often dubbed as **exigence** (Bitzer, 1968: 6). Swales (1990) presents a hierarchy of four types of exigences that helps scholars create a niche for writing.

First, readers may identify a **continuation exigence** where researchers follow the existing framework to make the previous study better. For instance, by applying the same research instrument to the same research site with a similar subject population designed in Chen (1993), Chen and Yang (2010) report a quasi-longitudinal study that accounts for the diachronic change of Chinese compliment responses over time. The replicated study finds that Chinese students changed their preferred compliment response from rejection to acceptance, indicating how the influx of Western culture changes Chinese people's behavior.

Second, scholars could further advance an academic inquiry by raising a **question exigence** that addresses an important question that has not been asked yet. In Haugh (2018: 157), facing diversified theories of (im)politeness, the author raises an essential question about "what do different theories allow us to see". Haugh interrogates the explanatory power of different theories, advocating a new direction of conducting meta-theorization of (im)politeness. In this case, instead of following one analytical framework and making the existing study better, the author opens up a different question to stimulate new studies.

Third, one could also manage to locate a **gap exigence** where the researcher can fill an empty space in knowledge. For example, the study on the Chinese online discourse marker *hehe* (Wang, 2012) stirred a sensation because no one has systematically analyzed discourse markers in cyberspeak. Indeed, addressing this exigence requires the author to conduct an exhaustive literature review about all the existing research available. Beginners often feel upset when they find that their "brilliant idea" has been heavily discussed long ago. Therefore, scholars strive to discover a knowledge gap by applying new language materials in new contextual settings, or from new analytical perspectives. For instance, adopting Neo-Gricean pragmatics, Huang (2018) analyzes an increasingly heated language phenomenon called "unarticulated constituent" that refers to a type of propositional constituent that is straightly communicated but not linguistically represented (e. g. , stating "I'm ready" without explicitly stating what I am ready for). Combined with rigorous analysis, this new theoretical perspective helps Professor Huang publish the article in an internationally renowned SSCI journal.

Finally, scholars should aim to reach **correction exigence**: pointing out that the previous methods, results, or arguments are incorrect and offering solutions to right the wrong. Some of the quintessential examples are the criticism of Grice's Cooperative Principle in Chapter Four, Austin's Speech Act Theory in Chapter Five, and Brown and Levinson's Politeness Strategies in Chapter Six. The identification of the loopholes in other's theory requires extreme caution and should not make blatant claims before fully understanding the "flawed theories".

7.1.2 Review articles and bibliographies

Bearing the above four types of exigences in mind, we begin to explore three major ways of literature mining. First, the most traditional method is through reading review articles and bibliography of academic works. By reading review articles, beginners will be able to have a quick sketch of a particular research area. At the end of the paper, there is always a section pointing out the research gaps among the existing studies and potentials for future studies. These gaps, though often tend to be general, are signposts of main directions that we beginners could work on. The specific research question, nevertheless, only emerges via intensive readings by researchers themselves.

When identifying an interesting exigence in the review article, we could refer to the relevant references listed at the end of the paper. Then, by reading these cited literatures and their references, we would gradually develop a sense of what-is-going-on in one particular research area. This process is made much easier through the **citing document** function from citation databases. This allows us to pin down the more updated literature germane to that present article we are reading. For example,

(7.1)   《语用三律》的引证文献:

中国学术期刊网络出版总库　　共 9 条
[1] 语用经济与语用优选:以方向推理为例[J]. 王茂. 浙江外国语学院学报. 2017(03)
[2] "新经济原则"与商务英语信函的言语优化配置[J]. 刘永厚,王园. 上海对外经贸大学学报. 2016(05)
[3] 商务英语语言的新经济原则[J]. 许佳,杨连瑞. 语言教育. 2014(04)

中国博士学位论文全文数据库　　共 3 条
[1] 语义缺省的认知拓扑研究[D]. 赵耿林. 西南大学 2016
[2] 基于英汉语料的仿拟跨学科研究[D]. 罗胜杰. 上海外国语大学 2014
[3] 中国法庭调解话语博弈研究[D]. 柯贤兵. 华中师范大学 2012

中国优秀硕士学位论文全文数据库　　共 11 条
[1] "一X一Y"格式研究[D]. 张艳杰. 扬州大学 2017
[2] 省力原则在兰州市口腔医院口译实践中的应用研究[D]. 叶挺挺. 兰州大学 2017
[3] 汉语全量对举构式群"要A有/没/就A, 要B有/没/就B"研究[D]. 自然. 湘潭大学 2015

中国重要会议论文全文数据库　　共 1 条
[1] 从语用三律分析《人人都爱雷蒙德》的幽默[A]. 梁小晏. 厦门大学外文学院第八届研究生学术研讨会论文集[C]. 2015

Example (7.1) displays the citing documents for Xiang's 2008 article *Three laws in speech behaviors*. We could find all the articles, doctoral dissertations, master theses, and important conference proceedings that cited Xiang (2008). This function could help us make clear a line of research following one leading publication. For the author himself, this function is instrumental to understanding how his article has been perceived by the research community, enabling scholars to revise their theories and engage with others. Similar functions can also be found on other search engines and databases such as Google Scholar and Web of Science.

7.1.3　Search engines and databases

After getting familiar with a research area, we start to collect existing studies targeted at a specific topic. The two essential components in this set of toolkit are academic search engines and databases. Below is a list of commonly used research engines in pragmatics①:

(7.2) Search engines

Search engines	Website
Google Scholar	https://scholar.google.com/
Microsoft Academic	https://academic.microsoft.com
百度学术	http://xueshu.baidu.com
360 学术	http://xueshu.so.com

In (7.2), Google Scholar is, without doubt, the most widely used search engine worldwide. It contains a wide range of scholarly publications such as books, journal articles, conference proceedings, preprints, theses, and dissertations in a variety of languages (Google Scholar, 2018). Its high coverage of the literature is supported by three algorithms: first, it contains a default logical AND between two words, viz. the results include all the words appear both together and separately in the literature; second, the range of search extends to all the available full texts of the literature; third, the searching results are case insensitive and derivation inclusive that all different forms of the keyword will be searched on Google Scholar.

Microsoft Academic features more sorting options and more diversified visualizations than Google Scholar (Zhao & Chen, 2014). Therefore, it can provide readers with a more globalized network among scholars in terms of their cooperation, citation, and academic influence, etc.

The two domestic search engines *BaiDuXueShu* and *360 XueShu* also have user-friendly interfaces and can easily yield a large amount of literature (See Liu, 2014; Xie & Guo, 2017 for more detailed comparisons between different search engines).

The second important source is academic databases, which are often supported by research institutions and academic publishers. They index a variety of publications include journal articles, theses, dissertations,

---

① In addition, a newly released search engine called Semantic Scholar deserves special attention. Based on deep learning and machine learning, Semantic Scholar provides a dynamic view of scholarships and helps generate an evaluative index of the influence of a particular publication, i.e., to that extent this paper is cited and how important this citation is (Xie & Guo, 2017). At present, this website only provides searches in computer science and medicine. However, we believe that in the near future, they will also include literatures in linguistics and pragmatics, making a larger contribution to the research community.

conference proceedings, books, and edited volumes. Some commonly used databases are listed below:

(7.3) Databases

Databases	Website(2022－6－10)
ScienceDirect	https://www.sciencedirect.com
Scopus	https://www.scopus.com
Web of Science	http://apps.webofknowledge.com
JSTOR	http://www.jstor.org
ProQuest	https://www.proquest.com
OSO	http://www.oxfordscholarship.com
LoC	http://catalog.loc.gov
CSSCI	http://cssci.nju.edu.cn
中国知网	http://www.cnki.net
维普期刊	http://lib.cqvip.com
万方数据	http://g.wanfangdata.com.cn/index.html
百链云图书馆	http://www.blyun.com

In general, databases consist of **full-text databases** and **citation databases**. As the names imply, the former contains the full content of the publication and the latter only includes citation information and sometimes the abstract. The full-text databases listed above are ScienceDirect, JSTOR, CSSCI, *ZhongGuoZhiWang*, *WeiPuQiKan*, *WanFangShuJu*. Among these, ScienceDirect indexes a large number of high-quality SSCI journals such as *Journal of Pragmatics*, *Language and Communication*, *Language Sciences*, and *Lingua*. *ZhongGuoZhiWang* and *WanFangShuJu* are two leading Chinese databases that provide a huge volume of journal articles, conference proceedings, theses, and dissertations.

Citation databases include Scopus, Web of Science, ProQuest, and *BaiLianYunTuShuGuan*. Among these, Scopus is the largest database under this category that ensures a comprehensive coverage of relevant literature. The SSCI and A&HCI articles indexed in the Web of Science core collection can provide high-quality research. Though *BaiLianYun* does not upload full texts on its server, we can request for a copy of the scholarly work from member libraries.

In addition, Oxford Scholarship Online (OSO) and the Library of Congress (LoC) are two important sources for published books. Library of Congress, in particular, has a huge collection of books because the U.S. law states that every book published in the US must submit two copies to LoC (Sun & Zhou, 2011: 56).

While both search engines and databases have been updating themselves to aim at a faster searching speed, higher accuracy, and larger coverage, they are still distinctive in three ways. First, most of the search engines can only provide basic search with very limited sorting criteria, whereas databases offer advanced search with a lot of selection categories and personalized search using regular expressions. Second, search engines, notably Google Scholar, apply a "soft AND" that often omits trivial words, but databases usually employ a "hard AND" that only includes precise matching (Zhai, 2015). Third, online search engines often fail to collapse the same literature in one title because it captures literature from a variety of sources and the different formatting of these sources fools the system to list them as separate entries. In contrast, since the compilation of a database follows a rather unified standard, there are few repeated entries shown in the result.

7.1.4 Bibliometric analysis and knowledge visualization

While pinpointing literature through manual reading and keywords search could yield a clear map of the present research landscape, they are still not sufficient to discover the internal linkage between different scholarships and unearth all possible research potentials. Bibliometric analysis provides us with an updated tool to acquire a clearer and more comprehensive understanding of the past, the present, and the future of a research area. Researchers could analyze the results manually (e.g., Sun, 2015) or use software such as CiteSpace (Li & Chen, 2017) and Jigsaw (Stasko et al, 2008). This section mainly introduces the growing trend of using CiteSpace for literature review.

Guided by Kuhn's (1962) iterative view of scientific revolutions, CiteSpace[①] is a Java-based knowledge visualization tool designed by Professor Chaomei Chen from Drexel University (Li & Chen, 2017: 2). Its main function is to "[detect] and [visualize] emerging trends and transient patterns in scientific literature" in a visualized manner (Chen, 2006: 359). This section focuses on two salient features of CiteSpace, and the detailed instructions can be found in Chen (2017) and Li and Chen (2017).

First, CiteSpace can visualize the distribution of a particular type of research information, including authors, countries, institutions, co-occurring keywords, co-occurring terms, overlapping sources of publication, co-occurring subject categories, co-citation, co-cited authors, co-cited journals, citing papers, and grant acknowledgments. Below is the landscape of the co-occurring keywords for SSCI publications of pragmatics from 2000 to 2018:

---

① Free download linkage: http://cluster.ischool.drexel.edu/~cchen/citespace/download/(2021-11-23)

Research Methods

(7.4) Co-occurring keywords for "pragmatics"

```
CiteSpace, v. 5.1.R8 SE (64-bit)
June 9, 2018 3:53:45 PM CST
WoS: /Users/James/Desktop/Pragmatics Undergraduate Edition/Pragmatics data/data
Timespan: 2000-2018 (Slice Length=2)
Selection Criteria: Top 50 per slice, LRF=-1, LBY=-1, e=1.0
Network: N=205, E=500 (Density=0.0239)
Largest CC: 201 (98%)
Nodes Labeled: 0.0%
Pruning: MST
```

organization
grammaticalization
relevance theory implicature speaker
identity discourse marker prosody
inference relevance communication pronoun
french context politeness strategy
comprehension english request
conversation analysis semantics pragmatics autism
irony discourse
grammar children language speech act
chinese
learner syntax acquisition adult
intonation focus conversation face mind
impoliteness spanish speech german
impairment japanese

Example (7.4) displays the most frequently occurring keywords in pragmatics from 2000 to 2018. The size and the darkness of the nodes are proportional to their occurrence in this time range. The bigger the size, the more frequent it occurs. A quick sketch could show us that pragmatics concerns the study of discourse, politeness, speech act, conversation, context, implicature, and identity in languages such as English, Japanese, Chinese, Spanish, and French. These groups of information would be conducive to our beginners to get familiar with the essential theories, heated topics, language of investigated, methodologies applied, laying a firm foundation for further inquiries.

Second, after locating a specific research topic, we can use CiteSpace to map out its different schools of thought through **cluster analysis**. Each cluster "represents the intellectual base of the underlying specialty" (Chen, 2017: 8). On the basis of these clusters, users can look closely into the specific references via cited documents and citing documents. The **cited documents** of A are those references article A itself cited, and the **citing documents** of B refer to those publications that cite B in their references. Hence, the accumulated cited references of a research area reflect its knowledge foundation and its citing references signal its emerging trend (Li & Chen, 2017: 174). Examples (7.5) and (7.6) show the citing articles and cited articles of the two biggest clusters in politeness research:

(7.5) Cited and citing documents for cluster 0

(7.6) Cited and citing documents for cluster 1

In each picture, the upper column is the list of clusters identified by CiteSpace. The lower left column displays the citing articles of a cluster and the lower right section shows the cited references of this cluster. By analyzing the cited references, we find that the cluster represents the classical study of politeness and cluster 1 embodies the postmodernist approach to politeness. Then, by carefully going through their citing articles, we conclude that future studies could be dedicated to bridging the gap between theoretical analysis and authentic interaction, advancing metatheorization of (im) politeness, investigating situated variations in its full embodiment, and utilizing the instrumentality of developed theories.

To sum up, CiteSpace provides detailed networking among different literatures and helps scholars to identify research trends and foci. What we have introduced is only the tip of an iceberg, and there is still a huge bulk of functions waiting for further exploration. For reference purposes, below is a list of applications of CiteSpace in pragmatics studies: an overview of pragmatics (Xiang, 2015), critical discourse analysis (Mu & Ma, 2016), interlanguage pragmatics (Yuan & Liu, 2017), relevance theory (Zhao & Xiang, 2018), grammaticalization (Yang & Xiang, 2018), and metaphor using the corpus method (Xue & Xiang, 2018), etc.

7.2 Data collection

After mining the literature, we begin to address the research exigence we identified among the existing studies. How to collect reliable and valid data largely determines the quality of our studies. Kasper and Dahl (1991: 217) note that data are collected on a **comprehension-production** continuum. Moving from the comprehension pole to the production pole, this section introduces five basic methods of data collection: interviews, questionnaires, discourse completion tests, role plays, and recordings[①]. The final part of this section presents three more trending methods advanced by cognitive psychology and computer technology.

7.2.1 Interviews

Interviews include structured, unstructured, or open-ended and semi-structured interviews (Sun & Zhou, 2011: 134). In **structured interviews**, researchers usually have prepared a list of questions and ask these questions in order. Since the questions are standard, the results are often used for quantitative research. In contrast, **unstructured interviews** do not have fixed questions and are designed to uncover the language use of the interviewee. In between, **semi-structured interviews** contain a guideline of questions but retain a degree of freedom to the interviewees.

Interviews have three advantages when carried out when conducted using audio or video recordings (Wray et al., 1998: 182). First, this allows the interviewers to free themselves from choosing what to take notes and what not to, helping them to concentrate on the content of the participants. Second, leaving the notes behind provides a more natural conversational environment that is conducive for the interviewees to process the questions. Third, researchers can collect these data without being influenced by their cursory writings.

Nevertheless, it also exposes three barriers. First, the transcription of data is time-consuming, especially for conversation analysis[②]. Researchers

---

[①] Other methods include intuition, introspection, oral report, field notes, diaries, observations, experiments, corpus data, etc.

[②] Some companies have developed software that can automatically transcribe audio and video recordings in texts. Some common examples include *kedaxunfei* (https://www.iflyrec.com, 2021−11−20) and *Descript* (https://www.descript.com, 2021−11−20).

need to write down the whole speech and with proper annotations. It is important to conduct the interview in a quiet place to avoid unnecessary background noise. Second, for unstructured and semi-structured interviews, the interviewer has to be trained to elicit data from the interviewees. In many cases, it means that the researchers have to carry out these interviews by themselves, making the study more time-consuming. Third, there is a potential variable that the participants' responses may be subject to the characteristics of the interviewer. For instance, if the participant is the roommate with the interviewer, he or she may use language differently from that of strangers.

For further explication, below is an application of unstructured interview in a published journal article discussing the discursive approach to (im)politeness:

> (7.7) *After having selected an extract, we then interviewed the four participants separately to find out how they evaluated the interaction. All participants were asked to listen to the recording and were given a transcript of the interaction before they were asked to give an evaluation of the situation.*
>
> (van der Bom & Mills, 2015: 194)

In the above case, the authors argue that politeness is not inherent in words and is subject to individual judgment (van der Bom & Mills, 2015). By setting up the above interview, they find that participants have different interpretations of their linguistic performances, supporting their hypothesis.

7.2.2 Questionnaires

In pragmatics, questionnaires are often used to assess language users' perception or comprehension of a particular subject. The two commonly used methods are **rating tasks** and **multiple-choice questions**. Both formats consist of a vignette description of a scenario and followed by some questions; the former is followed by a 3-point, 5-point, or 7-point scale to measure how appropriate a speech act is in the scenario, whereas the latter provides a number of possible speech acts and the examinees are asked to choose the most appropriate one (Hong, 2005: 43, 49). To improve the validity and the reliability of the questionnaires, we need to ensure that the test subjects match our research question and are represented evenly (e.g., age span when investigating how age affects the performance of a speech act). Before sending out the questionnaires, a pilot study on a small scale can help us to identify the loopholes in our design and revise it accordingly.

Below is an example of using rating tasks to measure the appropriateness of compliment responses between Chinese and English native speakers:

Chapter 7
Research Methods

(7.8) *The questionnaire comprised five scenarios, all of which contained a compliment on someone's performance/achievement, such as coming top in an examination...*

For each scenario, five different responses were listed: two acceptance responses, two rejection responses, and one deflection response...

Respondents were asked to evaluate each of the responses in terms of appropriateness, conceit, and [the] impression conveyed (favourable/bad). Three 5-point Likert-type rating scales were listed under each compliment response, and respondents were asked to circle the numbers on these scales that corresponded to their reactions to that response...

Chinese and English versions of the questionnaire were produced through the collaborative efforts of six bilingual speakers, who carefully checked the developing versions of the questionnaire for equivalence of meaning. Using the decentring process suggested by Brislin ... the scenarios and the responses were modified, until all parties have agreed on Chinese and English versions that were both acceptable and equivalent in meaning.

(Spencer-Oatey, Ng & Dong, 2008: 100—101)

From (7.8), we could observe that the rating task is contextualized in complimenting someone for his or her top examination score. Each scenario contains five speech acts that need to be evaluated on a 5-point scale. To address the validity and reliability of the test, the authors also specifically describe how the Chinese and English versions are matched and acceptable to all parties.

A modification of the research question can make (7.8) into a design for multiple choice questions. For instance, if the researchers want to investigate the pragmatic competence between native English speakers and EFL (English as Foreign Language) speakers, they could use the compliment scenario above and ask examinees to choose the most appropriate answer from the five listed responses. Then, by analyzing the choices between the two groups of speakers, they could find out to what extent the home culture influences the pragmatic competence in a learned culture. Nevertheless, Leech (2014: 250) notes that multiple-choice questions and its variants went out of fashion in the 1990s for their restricted coverage of pragmatic competence. It is still a valid measurement but needs to be used with caution.

7.2.3 Discourse completion tests

Discourse completion tests or discourse completion tasks (DCTs) were devised by Levenston and Blum (1978) and then adapted by Blum-Kulka (1982) to study requests in Hebrew. It is an incomplete written discourse sequence that requires participants to provide a response to address a specific scenario in a particular context. Below is an example used to elicit compliment response among Chinese college students:

(7.9) 说明:请就以下情景做出回应,对于每一种情景,您可能会发现好几种回应在社交方面均适当。如果是这样,请在画线部分写下所有这些回应。

1. 您遇见一位已有一段时间没有见面的熟人,互致问候之后,他/她说:"你真潇洒/漂亮,比上次见面的时候还要潇洒/漂亮。"您对此的回应是:
   A: _____
   B: _____
   C: _____
   D: _____

(Chen & Yang, 2010: 1961—1962, with adaptions of format and font)

While DCT is convenient to harvest a large amount of data and effectively control the variables (Hong, 2005: 61), it also faces heavy criticisms regarding the authenticity of the data (Leech, 2014: 252). First, the written questions entail the imaginary nature of the conversation that may not authentically reflect interlocutors' verbal encounters. In (7.9), the students have to imagine what they will do to respond to the compliment; in reality, however, they may be very likely to do otherwise. One solution is to use audios or videos to provide test scenarios that simulate real-life interactions.

Second, the limited space of DCT dictates the length of the response. Since Chen and Yang's (2010) study only leaves one line for each response, students will try to limit their answers in one line of texts. However, if the researcher chooses to leave a larger space, students then tend to fill in the empty space with lots of words, as they were told when preparing for the Chinese Gaokao. One potential solution is to upload the entire test on the Internet where the space for response grows as the respondent writes.

7.2.4 Role plays

Role play, sometimes dubbed as oral DCT, is one endeavor to balance the above predicament between the authenticity of data and the manipulation of variables. It is defined as "participation in simulated social situations that are

Chapter 7
Research Methods

intended to throw light upon the role/rule contexts governing 'real' life social episodes" (Cohen, Manion & Morrison, 2000: 370). In general, role plays can be divided into **open role play** and **closed role play** (Kasper & Dahl, 1991). The former only sets the initial situation, the actors' roles and their communicative goals and the latter also dictates the outcome of the interactions. Below is an open role play designed to elicit request data from American learners of Spanish:

 (7.10) *Role-play requests*
  Student-Professor: Asking for a letter of recommendation
  Imagine that you are in a Spanish-speaking country of your preference. You are in the final year of your undergraduate studies and you have decided to ask your Spanish professor, Professor "X", to write you a letter of recommendation. You have been a good student in the class and although your professor has always treated everyone equally, you're sure that he wouldn't have any reason not to write a letter for you. You prefer that the letter be written by this professor because this class has been an important one for your major and the material is representative of classes you have taken toward your major. The relationship between you and your professor is strictly academic and you have only interacted with each other at the University either in class or during office hours. You need the letter of recommendation and you go to his office to ask him to write you one. What do you say?

              (Félix-Brasdefer, 2007: 280)

In (7.10), the author created a scenario where participants need to use Spanish to ask for a recommendation letter. By comparing the performance between speakers with different levels of proficiency and contrasting them with other scenarios designed in this study, the researcher could uncover the developmental patterns of these language learners, contributing to the study of interlanguage pragmatics.

 The main advantage of role play, particularly open role play, is that it provides analysts with near-authentic data and the full discourse context of a particular speech event (Hong, 2005: 77). On the contrary, one practical shortcoming is that it requires a lot of manual work to transcribe and code the data (Leech, 2014: 254). Consequently, it is hard for researchers to collect a larger amount of data to even the insufficient representativeness of a small sample.

7.2.5 Recordings

We could also use **audio** and **video** taping equipment to record more authentic data. Heritage (1991: 238) notes that recordings can expand the range and enhance the precision of the data available; it also allows other researchers to have direct access to these firsthand data to help avoid personal bias in the analysis. When collecting these data, it is very important to note the underlying ethics and legality that researchers have to gain the permission of the participants (Wray et al., 1998: 154). This may raise the **observer's paradox** (Kasper & Dahl, 1991) that the participants' behavior will be affected by knowing that they are being watched. One solution is to only inform the participants they will be recorded but do not reveal the exact timing of the recordings. Here is an example:

(7.11) ①语料收集人得到观察对象的同意,在接下来的一学年中观察记录其在宿舍内的语言使用行为,作研究语料之用。为避免录音行为潜在的影响,保证会话的真实性,每次录音前不再告知观察对象将进行录音;②在开始阶段,语料收集人每天录制一段宿舍谈话,包括收集人缺席或者作为旁听者在场两种情况,重点关注被观察对象相互之间发起恭维时的恭维回应;③语料收集人将录音中的恭维和恭维回应语料进行转写,按照外貌、所属物、性格品质、能力和成就四个主题分类。

(Xia, Yin & Lan, 2017: 689)

The above case explains the data collection procedure in a study of Chinese compliment responses. By informing the participants one year ahead, the study addresses both the authenticity of the data and the legality of recording.

The choice between audio and video recording depends on the specific research question. If the study only focuses on the verbal aspect of speech, audio recording is both sufficient and convenient to elicit data. In recent years, the rise of multimodal analysis (Jewitt, 2009; Streeck, 2009; Zhu, 2006) boosts the need for visual data. By compositionally analyzing both verbal and non-verbal language, we could gain a more comprehensive understanding of interlocutors' meaning-making process.

7.2.6 Trending methods

What we have introduced above are the most basic methods of data collection in pragmatics. In recent years, there is a growing trend to use authentic data over elicited data (Ishihara, 2010; Leech, 2014) and the development of new methods brought informed by experimental pragmatics (Noveck & Sperber, 2005), Internet pragmatics (Yus, 2011), and corpus pragmatics (Aijmer & Rühlemann, 2015).

Chapter 7
Research Methods

The rise of experimental pragmatics gives birth to collecting data through psycholinguistic experiments (Gibbs, 2005). From the previous chapter, we get to know that pragmatics concerns the study of the meaning-making process, especially how people infer the pragmatically enriched meaning that has not been stated semantically. Therefore, scholars represented by Grice, Levinson, Horn, and Sperber and Wilson came up with different solutions to account for the meaning-making mechanism in our brain (see Sections 4.3 and 4.4). However, their theories, though insightful and self-contained, cannot be testified in real-world usages. Joining forces with psycholinguistics, experimental pragmatics enables researchers to indirectly observe how our brain functions through ERP (Evoked Response Potentials), fMRI (Functional Magnetic Resonance Imaging), eye tracking, etc. This interdisciplinary trend requires our beginners to explore not only the essential topics in pragmatics but also related knowledge.

The second trending method is to harvest data from cyberspace. Yus (2011) notes that online communication offers a distinct interpersonal relation between the addresser and the addressee and may lead to brand new choices of communicative strategies. Computer-mediated communication forms salient contrast with face-to-face communication over asynchronicity online versus synchronicity offline, task-orientation versus relation-orientation, anonymity versus familiarity, and longevity versus temporality (Graham & Hardaker, 2017). These distinctive features are conducive to interrogating and revising the existing theories. More importantly, online data are authentic and easy to retrieve. This saves our researchers from the treadmill job of transcribing and coding. Nevertheless, online data are not sufficient to explain all kinds of problems and should be used with caution: researchers need to consider to what extent the heterogeneousness of the online users will affect the result of the study or how to control these variations.

Third, the marriage between corpus linguistics and pragmatics gives birth to an emerging discipline of corpus pragmatics that produces both qualitative and quantitative analysis at the same time (Rühlemann & Aijmer, 2015: 12). By extracting data from pragmatically annotated corpus, researchers are able to draw their conclusions with a much lower risk of hasty generalization and do not have to superstitiously note in their limitations that their data size is too small to generalize. In the meantime, these annotations ensure that the pragmatic meaning worked out in each entry is contextualized and has been treated individually, catering to the contextual sensitivity in pragmatics. This approach, however, is still facing three challenges (see Leech, 2014). First, to complete annotating an entire corpus, even a small one, requires a heavy workload by a number of researchers. This calls for collaboration between different researchers and the rewarding could be substantial: scholars can use one corpus to produce a huge number of studies in many areas of pragmatics. While the first challenge is still manageable, the second is paradoxically unattainable: the annotation could be inconsistent when finished by multiple researchers because each of them may hold different interpretations of a single phenomenon. We hope this paradox could be solved by advancing semi-automatic or even full-automatic annotation that is guided by unified principles. Finally, sometimes, we could not exhaust all the necessary examples of a complied corpus and have to rely on introspection and field observation, etc. For instance, when describing the composite of Chinese vocatives in section 2.4, we find that the CLL corpus can only identify a small portion of their possible semantic representations. More complicated forms such as VP + de, *nizhege* + evaluative terms/titles are never found in the 4-million-word-corpus but are widely used in our daily lives. This indicates that our data should not be constrained to only one method and the combination of different methods could better contribute to our research.

7.3 Analytical methods

After gathering sufficient data for the identified exigence, we move to come up with solutions to explain our findings. The data we gathered can be either qualitative or quantitative. The distinction between these two types of data is that the **qualitative** data are nonnumerical and **quantitative** numerical (Babbie, 2013: 24). This section begins with some basic concepts in data analysis and then introduces three commonly used qualitative and quantitative methods of analysis: conversation analysis, discourse analysis, and statistical analysis.

7.3.1 Conversation analysis and discourse analysis

Conversation analysis (CA) is defined as the study that discovers the linguistic features of these naturally occurring conversations. Its precursors are American sociologist Harvey Sacks and his assistant Emanuel Schegloff. In the 1960s, while working at the Center for the Scientific Study of Suicide, they noticed that the calls made to the center share similar patterns and began to systematize their openings (Schegloff, 1968) and closings (Schegloff & Sacks, 1973). These two articles map out the central tenet and research methodology of conversation analysis, manifesting its interactive nature and the tendency to analyze conversation structure globally (Yu, 2008: 5). The main body of this section elaborates on four essential analytical concepts in conversation analysis: turning-taking, adjacent pairs, preference organization, and presequence.

Chapter 7
Research Methods

Turn-takings

When Mr. Donald Trump won the presidential election in 2016, we knew that it was Trump rather than his rival Mrs. Hillary Clinton who would have the right to speak at the inaugural address. This right to speak is called the **floor** and having control of it is termed as a **turn** (Yule, 1996: 72). And only one person can hold the floor at a particular turn. **Turn-taking**, consequently, refers to the shift of this control from one speaker to another. And the point where this shift occurs is called **transition relevant places** or TRPs. Let's illustrate this with the following examples:

(7.12) *A moderator is hosting a talk show with three guests:*
  Moderator: Welcome to today's program. Today's topic is GM food. And let's talk about the pros and cons it may have.
  (4 seconds)
  Guest C: I'll say something first. I don't think it would be a big problem.
  Guest A: I think there are too many unknown factors about it.
  Guest B: I think it depends ...

At first, it is the moderator who holds the floor. Guest C takes the next turn by saying that *I'll say something first*. In general, the TRPs are the ends of each complete sentence, as in from Guest C to Guest A and to Guest B.

To explain the mechanism of turn-taking, Sacks, Schegloff and Jefferson (1974) postulate two general rules: the first is that the current speaker selects the next speaker; the second is that the next speaker selects himself by himself. In conversation, the first rule is preferred over the second one. Therefore, the current speaker is required to select the next speaker during his own turn. Otherwise, it would generate a pause (a gap) after the speaker finishes. In scenario (7.12), the floor is left untaken for 4 seconds because the moderator did not select a specific speaker for the next turn. Levinson (1983: 302) suggests that listeners can signal their intention of speaking to the current speaker by actively gazing at the speaker. For instance, a student is very likely to be chosen to answer the question in class if he gazes at the teacher, or in most cases, just simple eye contact. If the question is very difficult, the teacher usually finds that most of the students will bury their heads between their arms, avoiding to being asked to take this challenge. And whoever pops their head up would be called upon immediately.

When the first rule is not applicable, the next rule is abided by. Guest C volunteers to share his opinion in (7.12). Others may also step in before the current speaker finishes his speech if the first speaker talks continuously and does not follow the first rule. This frequently occurs in political debates. For example,

(7.13) *In the third round of presidential debates between Barack Obama and John McCain in 2008, the moderator is Bob Schieffer*:
Obama: And I think Congressman Lewis' point was that we have to be careful about how we deal with our supporters. Now...
McCain: You've got to read what he said...
Obama: Let—let—let...
McCain: You've got to read what he said.
Obama: Let me—let me complete...
Schieffer: Go ahead.
Obama: ... my response. I do think...

In the above case, as indicated by ellipses, Mr. Obama was interrupted twice by Mr. McCain before the moderator granted the floor to Obama again. The phenomenon that both speakers attempt to say something simultaneously is called **overlap**. One may observe that McCain successfully interrupted Obama when he started a new sentence (*now*...). A useful technique practiced by politicians is to ignore the natural break that occurred at the end of each sentence; instead, they create breaks in the middle of the sentence, leaving fewer chances for others to take the floor (Mey, 2001: 139). Another commonly used strategy is to indicate a larger structure at the beginning of the speech (Yule, 1996: 75), as in (7.14)—(7.16).

(7.14) I have three arguments against your proposition. First...
(7.15) I'll spend two minutes introducing our project...
(7.16) Do you know about the Manhattan Project? It is...

In (7.14), the speaker indicates that he has three rebuttals, and his opponent will be more likely to retort after he has finished all three points. Example (7.15) suggests the time duration the speaker wants to occupy; therefore, the hearer usually will give the speaker two minutes before making responses. Finally, in (7.16), the speaker highlights the topic he is going to talk about; a cooperative listener will know the speaker ends his turn when he finishes talking about the Manhattan Project.

Moreover, the speaker can opt to stress the importance of the addressee listening to his speech. For example,

(7.17) You have to listen to what I say; it's about your investment. It is about...

In doing so, the speaker attracts the addressee's attention, being less likely to be interrupted and therefore holding the floor for a longer period. In fact, the effort of carefully listening to others is also seen as a communicative art to reduce misunderstandings, and this kind of rhetorical practice is called **listening-rhetoric** (see Booth, 2004).

Adjacent pairs

In our daily communication, speakers usually generate some automatic follow-ups to the previous turn. For example,

(7.18) —How you doin?
—Doin' good. And you?
(7.19) —You did an awesome job!
—Thanks, man.
(7.20) —We would like to invite you to our opening ceremony.
—I'd love to come.

In these examples, a greeting is followed by another greeting, a compliment binds with compliment response, and an invitation is responded by acceptance (or rejection). This mechanism of conversation organization is called **adjacency pairs**. An adjacency pair is considered as the basic unit of conversational organization (Coulthard, 2014: 70; Levinson, 1983: 304). Schegloff and Sacks (1973: 295—296) (see also Sacks, 1992) suggest five characterizations of an adjacency pair:

(7.21) a. It contains two utterances.
b. These two utterances are positioned adjacently.
c. These two utterances are produced by two different speakers.
d. It consists of a first part and a second part.
e. A particular first part creates a specific expectation of the second part.

The adjacency pair basically operates as follows: when a speaker produces the first part of a particular pair, he has to stop speaking; and the next speaker must respond immediately with the second half of that pair.

However, Schegloff and Sack's characterization also exposes several problems. First, adjacency pairs often do not strictly occur as exemplified in (7.18) — (7.20). In many cases, the speaker may insert another question before receiving the answer to the first question. This phenomenon is called **conditional relevance** (Merritt, 1976: 332). See the illustration below:

(7.22) **Customer**: Do you have computer chargers?   (Q1)
Salesperson: What kind of computer do you use?   (Q2)
Customer: It's a MacBook Air 2015.   (A2)
Salesperson: Yes, we have. It's $100.   (A1)

Instead of answering the customer directly, the salesperson asks a follow-up question to inquire about the type of computer model the customer uses. After getting the specifics of the type model, the salesperson responds to the initial question asked by the customer. And the embedded question-answer part is called an **insertion sequence** (Q2—A2 in 7.22).

Another problem is that the first part may correspond to a great many second parts (Levinson, 1983: 307). For instance, suppose Mary asks a question about conversational implicature to John. John could directly answer Mary's question. He could also direct Mary to another person if he thinks this question is too difficult to answer. Or he could refuse to answer Mary's question because he simply dislikes her. Among these three responses, what Mary most prefers is John answering her question directly. And what she most disprefers is John refusing to give her any information. This involves the concept of preference organization and will be elaborated on in the following part.

Preference organization

The central tenet of **preference organization** is that these potential second parts can be grouped into preferred and dispreferred categories of responses (Levinson, 1983: 307). The **preference** is not what an individual speaker expects; rather, it refers to what the society conventionally expects. Their general patterns are presented below (adapted from Levinson, 1983: 336 and Yule, 1996: 79).

(7.23) General patterns of preferred and dispreferred responses

First parts	Second parts	
	Preferred	Dispreferred
Assessment	Agreement	Disagreement
Blame	Denial	Admission
Invitation/Offer	Acceptance	Refusal/Declination
Proposal	Agreement	Disagreement
Question	Expected answer	Unexpected answer
Request	Acceptance	Refusal

These dispreferred seconds display several important features: first, they often contain more words than the preferred responses; second, the speaker may pause for a while before giving responses; third, the speaker tends to use filler words (e.g., uh, well,) or hedges (e.g., I don't really know, but...); fourth, the dispreferred responses often appear to be sound explanations (e.g., I really want to help you, but I'm afraid it goes beyond my reach); finally, the speaker may reply in an indirect way. The patterns for dispreferred seconds in Chinese are presented as follows (adapted from Yule, 1996: 81):

(7.24) Patterns for dispreferred seconds in Chinese

Patterns	Examples
Apology	实在抱歉,不好意思
Appeal for understanding	你也知道
Delay/Hesitate	(停顿),额,嗯
Express doubts	不知道了,我也不太清楚
Give an account	实在太忙,实在不行
Hedge the negative	或许,恐怕
Make it non-personal	大家都这样
Mention obligation	我还得……
Preface	这个嘛,哎呀,呀
Token appreciation	谢谢,感谢
Use mitigators	真的,实在是,着实

While the above analyses mainly focus on the maximally cooperative responses, Pomerantz (1975, 1984) points out that speakers often display degrees of agreement and disagreement with a second assessment. In general, an agreement can be assessed with the upgraded, the same evaluation, or the downgraded agreements and disagreements. An **upgraded agreement** employs a stronger evaluative term or an intensifier in the second assessment. For example,

(7.25) With stronger evaluative term
—I think Tom did a good job.
—He did an excellent job!

(7.26) With an intensifier
—Tim says he found some important evidence.
—Yes, he found some really important evidence.

A **same evaluation** is a case that the recipient repeats the speaker's original statement. Finally, a **downgraded agreement** is the weakened assessment compared to the prior one. Same evaluation and downgraded agreement are weak agreements and often time express disagreement and are called **agreement tokens**. For instance,

(7.27) —He didn't do well today.
—Yes, he didn't. But at least he tried very hard.

(7.28) —Durian is the queen of all fruits.
—Durian is tasty. I think strawberry is better.

In both (7.27) and (7.28), the recipients offer their different opinions after agreeing with the previous speaker.

In contrast, the speaker can also express their disagreements with the following delay devices: "no talks", request for clarification, partial repeats, and repair initiators (e. g. , what?; Hm?), and turn prefaces (e. g. , well) (Pomerantz, 1984: 70). These are illustrated in (7. 29)—(7. 33) respectively:

(7. 29) —Tom ruins the project.
(2 seconds)
—You know what? Tom is the most diligent person in the group.
(7. 30) —We should elect Jack as our class president.
—Do you mean the Jack who escapes classes all the time? Are you crazy?
(7. 31) —Mary looks pretty.
—She is pretty, but not according to my criterion.
(7. 32) —We learned that Grace proposed the Cooperative Principle.
—Hm?
—I said Grace proposed a theory called the Cooperative Principle.
—Boy, I think you meant Paul Grice, right?
—Sorry, I got it wrong.
(7. 33) —Could you lend me $200? I promise I'll pay you back tomorrow.
—Well, dude, you still haven't returned the $200 you borrowed last week.

Moreover, not all agreements are preferred and not all disagreements are dispreferred. A disagreement is often preferred if the speaker makes a self-depreciation evaluation (Pomerantz, 1975: 101). See the following illustration:

(7. 34) **Jane**: Am I getting fat?
Tom: Of course not, you are too skinny.
(7. 35) **Jack**: Do you think I'm a loser?
Jim: Are you kidding, man? You are the best in our class.

Finally, the exploitation of preferred and dispreferred responses can create humorous effects (Stokeo, 2008). Recalling the example we used to illustrate insertion sequence in (7. 22), the answer *It is a MacBook Air* can be considered as a preferred response. A dispreferred response, on the other hand, can be hilarious:

(7. 36) **Customer**: Do you have computer chargers?
Salesperson: What kind of computer do you use?
Customer: It's a white one.
Salesperson: …

In the above case, instead of describing the brand and the mode of his computer, the customer responds with an unexpected but somewhat related answer: *It's a white one*. The audience will find the answer funny when making a comparison with the preferred answer.

Presequences

Everyone must have experienced that the speakers usually feed some information related to their topic before engaging in the essential business. This additional information is called **presequence**. Typical examples are summons or attention-getters, such as *Hey*, *Excuse me*, vocatives (e. g. , man, dude, see Section 2.3.1), and *nin hao*, "hello", etc. Some other commonly used presequences are pre-announcements (e. g. , *You know what? Guess what I dug out?*), pre-invitations (e. g. , *Do you have plans tonight?*), pre-requests (e. g. , *Do you have your wallet with you?*), and pre-closings (e. g. , *okay, well, so*) (cf. Levinson, 1983: 346; Terasaki, 2004). These are illustrated in (7.37) — (7.40) respectively.

(7.37) Pre-announcement
John: You know what?
Mary: What did you get?
John: Trump just beat Clinton by a very small margin.
Mary: Are you serious?

(7.38) Pre-invitation
Tom: Do you have any plans tonight?
Mary: Not really.
Tom: I happen to have two tickets for a drama tonight. Do you wanna go with me?

(7.39) Pre-request
Franny: Do you have your wallet with you?
Dillon: What do you need?
Franny: Could you lend me $20?
Dillon: (*Taking out his wallet*) Here you are.

(7.40) Pre-closings
Christine and Gregory are chatting and it's getting late.
Christine: Yes, that's interesting... So...
Gregory: Okay. Well, I guess I'll see you around.
Christine: Sure. Good-bye.
Gregory: Bye.

It is worth noting that pre-request is often accompanied by the aforementioned insertion sequences. In (7.39), instead of directly answering Franny's question, Dillon initiates another question, asking about her needs. If Dillon is going for a trip and he often forgets his wallet, Franny's question could also serve as a reminder for Dillon. In this case, it is no longer a presequence of a request, but the main content of a particular turn.

In contrast to presequence, Liu and Yu (2018) propose a closely related concept of **goings-in-front-of-an-action** that also occurs before the base pair, but holds a loose logical relation with it. One common example is to make small talks at the beginning of the conversation. This type of sequence is interactively significant because it helps create a rapport conversational environment, naturally moving into the main content (ibid: 32).

In addition to CA, **discourse analysis** (DA) is another major approach to the examination of longer stretches of texts and the understanding of language beyond the sentence level. In general, DA is essentially a theoretical approach that sums up a number of basic categories and formulates a set of rules upon these categories. The common topics in DA are **information structure** (how given and new information are organized in discourse), **cohesion** (grammatical and lexical relatedness), **coherence** (logical consistency of the content), and **discourse markers** (a set of expressions that connects sentences but does not constitute the propositional meaning of these sentences) (Liu & Wen, 2006).

We close this part with a brief comparison between CA and DA. Generally speaking, there are two major distinctions between the two approaches. First, in terms of methodology, CA focuses on inducing the recurring patterns based on many instances of naturally occurring data, whereas DA attempts to give immediate categorization according to the limited data at hand. CA mostly derives systematic properties of talks from many instances of a particular phenomenon and DA tends to unveil "what really happened" in one particular occurrence. The second distinction is that CA values the interactional and inferential outcomes of different choices, but DA objects to this intuitive guess, focusing on the occurrences that actually happened. In other words, CA concentrates on sense-making, whereas DA displays diversified goals, such as establishing the factual status of an event, revealing the relevant mental states towards some social actions, or unearthing the development of ideologies.

7.3.2 Statistical analysis

After introducing the two common qualitative research methods in pragmatics, we move to elaborate on how to deal with numbers in pragmatics. The first step is to code our data and transfer them into numbers, for instance, the number of positive politeness and negative politeness strategies used when applying Brown and Levinson's theory or the number of people choosing different compliment responses listed in the questionnaire.

Based on the number of variables investigated simultaneously, quantitative data analyses include **univariate analysis** (on dependent variable), **bivariate analysis** (with two dependent variables), and **multivariate analysis** (with multiple dependent variables). Univariate analysis is used to describe the distribution and dispersion of the sample; bivariate analysis is applied to determine the relationship between these two variables; and multivariate analysis is designed to investigate the outcome of several variables, such as studying how age, gender and level of education influence people's choice of compliment responses and their evaluation of different responses(See Babbie, 2013: 418, 430, 434).

In most statistical analyses, we need to calculate the correlation between different variables. Ideally, we hope that the result of our small sample can represent the distribution of the larger population we study, as in interviewing 300 college students from four universities in Beijing to represent the population characteristics for a study of all university students in Beijing. Nevertheless, the correlation we computed may be erroneous due to the unrepresentativeness of our sample. For instance, we may choose a sample that uses more positive compliment responses than average or a group of students who intend to respond more negatively than the population. This is called **sampling error** and we use the **level of significance** to measure the degree of confidence we have in the relationship between different variables. A level of 0.05 significance indicates that there is only a 5% chance that we might falsely reject the null hypothesis because we made a mistake in collecting the sample. While this 0.05 is usually the minimum threshold for a legitimate association, researchers may set a more stringent threshold if they could not afford an error rate of 5%, such as in medical procedures. On the other hand, researchers may also set a more liberal threshold (larger than 0.05) if the study is exploratory in nature that tries to identify possible relationships between variables. In the remainder of this section, we present two commonly used methods to calculate correlation: **Chi-squared test** and **T-test**. Within limited space, we do not intend to go into the specifics of these tests, but to offer you their underlying mechanisms.

Essentially, chi square test is based on the **null hypothesis** that "there is no relationship between two variables in the total population" (Babbie, 2013: 475). It measures the discrepancy between the observed and the expected distributions of our sample and the probability that we could solely attribute this discrepancy to sampling error. The test result is jointly determined by the degree of freedom[①], the level of significance and the value of chi-squared statistic. If the value of chi square is higher than its threshold on a specific level of significance, say at 0.05, then we could conclude that the null hypothesis is 95% true that the discrepancy is only a result of sampling error. Otherwise, the difference must have been influenced by its internal relation in addition to the sampling error. In other words, if we find the value of chi square is lower than the threshold at 0.05, then we can conclude that at least a 95% chance that the variables are related.

T-test is often used to test the correlation of variables in smaller samples. It is commonly used to compute the statistical significance of differences in group means. Sharing a similar logic, we calculate the value of T-test and then compare it to its threshold at a specific level of significance. To close up this section, we would like to bring about one more caveat: While tests of significance offer us objective data of to what extent the result helps us infer the relationship of variables, it does not entail any causal relationship between the two variables. We researchers still need to provide logical arguments to identify the underlying reasons for the association.

7.4 Review

- **Literature mining**
  - Four types of exigences
    - Continuation exigence
    - Question exigence
    - Gap exigence
    - Correction exigence
  - Review articles and bibliographies
  - Search engines and databases
    - E.g. ScienceDirect, Google Scholar, Web of Science
  - Bibliometric analysis and knowledge visualization
    - E.g. CiteSpace, Carrot2
- **Data collection**
  - Types of data collection
    - Comprehension
    - Production

[①] The degree of freedom refers to the variation for possibility for a statistical model. It is computed as follows: $df = (c-1) * (r-1)$. df stands for degrees of freedom; c stands for the number of columns in the observed chart and r means that of the rows. For example, in an observed chart of 2 by 2, the degree of freedom is 1.

- Interviews
  - Structured interviews
  - Unstructured or open-ended interviews
  - Semi-structured interviews
- Questionnaires
  - Rating tasks
  - Multiple choice questions
- Discourse completion tests
  - Written DCTs
  - Oral DCTs
- Role plays
  - Open role play
  - Closed role play
- Recordings
  - Audio recordings
  - Video recordings

Analytical methods
- Types of analysis
  - Qualitative analysis
  - Quantitative analysis
- Conversation analysis
  - Turning-taking
  - Adjacent pair
  - Preference organization
  - Presequence
- Discourse analysis
  - Information structure
  - Cohesion
  - Coherence
  - Discourse marker
- Statistical analysis
  - Level of significance
  - Chi-squared
  - T-test

References

Aijmer, K. 2013. *Understanding Pragmatic Markers: A Variational Pragmatic Approach*. Edinburgh: Edinburgh University Press.
Aijmer, K. 2015. Pragmatic markers. In K. Aijmer & C. Rühlemann (eds.), *Corpus Pragmatics*. 195—218. Cambridge: Cambridge University Press.
Aijmer, K. & Rühlemann, C. (eds.). 2015. *Corpus Pragmatics*. Cambridge: Cambridge University Press.
Allami, H. & Naeimi, A. 2011. A cross-linguistic study of refusals: An analysis of pragmatic competence development in Iranian EFL learners. *Journal of Pragmatics*, 43(1), 385—406.
Anderson, S. R. & E, Keenan. 1985. Deixis. In T. Shopen (ed.). *Language Typology and Syntactic Description*. 259—308. Cambridge: Cambridge University Press.
Anscombe, G. E. M. 1957. *Intention*. Oxford: Blackwell.
Ariel, M. 2010. *Defining Pragmatics*. Cambridge: Cambridge University Press.
Aristotle. 2007. *On Rhetoric* (2nd Edition) (G. A. Kennedy Trans.) New York: Oxford University Press.
Arundale, R. B. 2006. Face as relational and interactional: A communication framework for research on face, facework, and politeness. *Journal of Politeness Research*, 2(2), 193—216.
Arundale, R. B. 2010. Constituting face in conversation: Face, facework, and interactional achievement. *Journal of Pragmatics*, 42(8), 2078—2105.
Arundale, R. B. 2013. Face as a research focus in interpersonal pragmatics: Relational and emic perspectives. *Journal of Pragmatics*, 58(8), 108—120.
Astington, J. W. 1988. Children's understanding of the speech act of promising. *Journal of Child Language*, 15(1), 157—173.
Atlas, J. D. & Levinson, S. C. 1981. It-clefts, informativeness and logical form: Radical pragmatics (revised standard version). In P., Cole. (ed.). *Radical Pragmatics*. 1—62. New York: Academic Press.
Austin, J. L. 1962. *How to Do Things with Words*. Oxford: Oxford University Press.
Austin, J. L. 1975. *How to Do Things with Words* (2 nd Edition). Oxford: Oxford University Press.
Austin, P. 1990. Politeness revisited—the dark side. In A. Bell & J. Holmes. (eds.). *New Zealand Ways of Speaking English*, 277—293. Philadelphia: Multilingual Matters.
Babbie, E. 2013. *The Practice of Social Research* (13th Edition). Cambridge, MA: Wadsworth.
Bach, K. 1994. Conversational impliciture. *Mind & Language*, 9(2), 124—162.
Bach, K. 2005. Context *ex machina*. In Z., Szabó. (ed.). *Semantics versus Pragmatics*. 15—44. Oxford: Clarendon Press.
Bach, K. 2006. The top 10 misconceptions about implicature. In B. J., Birner & G. Ward (eds.) *Drawing the Boundaries of Meaning: Neo-Gricean Studies in Pragmatics and Semantics in Honor of Laurence R. Horn*. 21—30. Amsterdam: John Benjamins.
Bach, K. 2010. Implicature vs. explicature: What's the difference?. In B. Soria & E. Romero (eds.). *Explicit Communication: Robyn Carston's Pragmatics* 126—137. Basingstoke: Palgrave Macmillan.
Bach, K., & R., Harnish. 1979. *Linguistic Communication and Speech Acts*. Cambridge, MA: MIT Press.

Bar-Hillel, Y. 1971. Out of the pragmatic wastebasket. *Linguistic Inquiry*, 2(3), 401—407.
Ballmer, T., & Brennstuhl, W. 2013. *Speech Act Classification: A Study in the Lexical Analysis of English Speech Activity Verbs*. B150erlin: Springer.
Beaver, D. I. 2001. *Presupposition and Assertion in Dynamic Semantics*. Stanford: CSLI Publications.
Bella, S. 2012. Pragmatic development in a foreign language: A study of Greek FL requests. *Journal of Pragmatics*, 44(13), 1917—1947.
Bitzer, L. F. 1968. The rhetorical situation. *Philosophy & Rhetoric*, 1(1), 1—14.
Blum-Kulka, S. 1982. Learning how to say what you mean in a second language: A cross-cultural study of Hebrew and English. *Applied Linguistics*, 3, 29—59.
Blum-Kulka, S. 1987. Indirectness and politeness in requests: Same or different?. *Journal of Pragmatics*, 11(2), 131—146.
Blum-Kulka, S., & Olshtain, E. 1984. Requests and apologies: A cross-cultural study of speech act realization patterns CCSARP. *Applied Linguistics*, 5, 196—213.
Blum-Kulka, S., House, J., & Kasper, G. 1989. *Cross-Cultural Pragmatics: Requests and Apologies*. Norwood: Ablex Pub.
BMTN Staff, 2012 May 21. Couple exchanges wedding vows in a southern Minnesota cemetery. Retrieved from https://bringmethenews.com/news/couple-exchanges-wedding-vows-in-a-southern-minnesota-cemetery.
Booth, W. C. 2004. *The Rhetoric of RHETORIC: The Quest for Effective Communication*. Malden, MA: Blackwell.
Borg, E. 2004. *Minimal Semantics*. Oxford: Clarendon Press.
Bourdieu, P. 1990. *The Logic of Practice*. Stanford: Stanford University Press.
Bousfield, D. 2008. *Impoliteness in Interaction*. Amsterdam & New York: John Benjamins.
Brown, P. 2017. Politeness and impoliteness. In Huang, Y. (ed.). *The Oxford Handbook of Pragmatics*. 383—399. New York, NY: Oxford University Press.
Brown, R. & A. Gilman. 1960. The pronouns of power and solidarity. In T. Sebeok (ed.). *Aspects of Style in Language*. 253—276. Cambridge, MA: MIT Press.
Brown, P. & S. C. Levinson. 1978. Universals in language usage: Politeness phenomena. In E. N. Goody (ed.). *Questions and Politeness*. 56—310. Cambridge: Cambridge University Press.
Brown, P., & Levinson, S. C. 1987. *Politeness: Some Universals in Language Usage*. Cambridge: Cambridge University Press.
Byon, A. 2006. The role of linguistic indirectness and honorifics in achieving linguistic politeness in Korean requests. *Journal of Politeness Research*, 2(2), 247—276.
Campbell, P. N. 1973. A rhetorical view of locutionary, illocutionary, and perlocutionary acts. *Quarterly Journal of Speech*, 59(3), 284—296.
Cao, X. Q. 1986. *The Story of Stone*. (D. Hawkes Trans.). London: Penguin. (Original work published 1760).
Cappelen, H. & E. Lepore. 2005. *Insensitive Semantics*. Oxford: Blackwell.
Carnap, R. 1942. *Introduction to Semantics*. Cambridge: Harvard University Press.
Carston, R. 2004. Review of Stephen C. Levinson's 'Presumptive Meanings: The Theory of Generalized Conversational Implicature'. *Journal of Linguistics*, 40(1), 181—186.
Carston, R. 2009. The explicit/implicit distinction in pragmatics and the limits of explicit communication. *International Review of Pragmatics*, 1, 35—62.
Chao, Y. R. 1965/2011. *A Grammar of Spoken Chinese*. Beijing: The Commercial Press.
Chen, C. M. 2006. Cite Space II: Detecting and visualizing emerging trends and transient

patterns in scientific literature. *Journal of the American Society for Information Science and Technology*, 57(3): 359—377.

Chen, C. M. 2017. Science mapping: A systematic review of the literature. *Journal of Data and Information Science*, 2(2), 1—40.

Chen, R. 1993. Responding to compliments: A contrastive study of politeness strategies between American English and Chinese speakers. *Journal of Pragmatics*, 20(1), 49—75.

Chen, R. 2001. Self-politeness: A proposal. *Journal of Pragmatics*, 33(1), 87—106.

Chen, R. & Yang, D. 2010. Responding to compliments in Chinese: Has it changed?. *Journal of Pragmatics*, 42(7), 1951—1963.

Chen, Y. S. 2015. Developing Chinese EFL learners' email literacy through requests to faculty. *Journal of Pragmatics*, 75, 131—149.

Chen, R., He, L. & Hu, C. 2013. Chinese requests: In comparison to American and Japanese requests and with reference to the "East-West divide". *Journal of Pragmatics*, 55, 140—161.

Cohen, T. 1973. Illocutions and perlocutions. *Foundations of Language*, 9(4), 492—503.

Cohen, L., Manion, L. & Morrison, K. 2000. *Research Methods in Education* (5th Edition). London & New York: Routledge.

Cummings, L. 2005. *Pragmatics: A Multidisciplinary Perspective*. London: Routledge.

Comrie, B. 1976. Linguistic politeness axes: speaker-addressee, speaker-reference, speaker-bystander. *Pragmatics Microfiche*, 1(7), A3—B1.

Coulthard, M. 2014. *An Introduction to Discourse Analysis*. (2nd Edition). London & New York: Routledge.

Croft, W. 1994. Speech act classification, language typology and cognition. In S. L. Tsohatzidis (ed.). *Foundations of Speech Act Theory: Philosophical and Linguistic Perspectives*. 460—477. London: Routledge.

Culpeper, J. 1996. Towards an anatomy of impoliteness. *Journal of Pragmatics*, 25(3), 349—367.

Culpeper, J. 2005. Impoliteness and entertainment in the television quiz show: The Weakest Link. *Journal of Politeness Research*, 1(1), 35—72.

Culpeper, J. 2008. Reflections on impoliteness, relational work and power. In D. Bousfield & M.A. Locher (eds.). *Impoliteness in Language: Studies on Its Interplay with Power in Theory and Practice*. 17—44. Berlin & New York: Mouton de Gruyter.

Culpeper, J. 2010. Conventionalised impoliteness formulae. *Journal of Pragmatics*, 42(12), 3232—3245.

Culpeper J. 2011. *Impoliteness: Using Language to Cause Offence*. Cambridge: Cambridge University Press.

Culpeper, J., Bousfield, D. & Wichmann, A. 2003. Impoliteness revisited: with special reference to dynamic and prosodic aspects. *Journal of Pragmatics*, 35(10—11), 1545—1579.

Culpeper, J., Haugh, M., & Kádár, D. Z. (eds.). 2017. *The Palgrave Handbook of Linguistic (Im)politeness*. London: Palgrave Macmillan.

Cummings, L. 2005. *Pragmatics: A Multidisciplinary Perspective*. Edinburgh: Edinburgh University Press.

Dascal, M. & Gross, A. G. 1999. The marriage of pragmatics and rhetoric. *Philosophy & Rhetoric*, 32(2), 107—130.

Davies, B. L. 2018. Evaluating evaluations: What different types of metapragmatic behaviour can tell us about participants' understandings of the moral order. *Journal of Politeness

Research, 14(1), 121—151.
Dynel, M. 2012. Swearing methodologically: The (im)politeness of expletives in anonymous commentaries on YouTube. *Journal of English Studies*, (10), 25—50.
Dynel, M. 2013. Impoliteness as disaffiliative humour in film talk. In M. Dynel (ed.). *Developments in Linguistic Humour Theory*. 105 — 144. Amsterdam & Philadelphia: John Benjamins.
Dynel, M. 2015. The landscape of impoliteness research. *Journal of Politeness Research*, 11(2), 329—354.
Eelen, G. 2001. *A Critique of Politeness Theories*. Manchester, UK; Northampton, MA: St. Jerome Pub.
Egner, I. 2006. Intercultural aspects of the speech act of promising: Western and African practices. *Intercultural Pragmatics*, 3(4), 443—464.
Fauconnier, G. 1985. *Mental spaces: Aspects of Meaning Construction in Natural Language*. Cambridge, MA: MIT Press.
Félix-Brasdefer, J. C. 2007. Pragmatic development in the Spanish as a FL classroom: A cross-sectional study of learner requests. *Intercultural Pragmatics*, 4(2), 253—286.
Fraser, B. 1990. Perspectives on politeness. *Journal of Pragmatics*, 14(2), 219—236.
Fraser, B. 1996. Pragmatic markers. *Pragmatics*, 6, 167—190.
Fraser, B. 2006. Towards a theory of discourse markers. In K., Fischer (ed.) *Approaches to Discourse Particles*. 189—205. The Netherlands: Elsevier.
Frege, G. 1892/1952. On sense and reference. In P. T. Geach & M. Black (eds.). *The Philosophical Writings of Gottlob Frege* (2nd Edition). 56—78. Oxford: Blackwell.
Fukushima, S. 1996. Request strategies in British English and Japanese. *Language Sciences*, 18(3), 671—688.
Gaines, R. N. 1979. Doing by saying: Toward a theory of perlocution. *Quarterly Journal of Speech*, 65(2), 207—217.
Gagné, N. O. 2010. Reexamining the notion of negative face in the Japanese Socio linguistic politeness of request. *Language & Communication*, 30(2), 123—138.
Gazdar, G. 1979. *Pragmatics: Presupposition, Implicature, and Logical Form*. London: Academic Press.
Gibbs, R. W. 2005. Psycholinguistic experiments and linguistic-pragmatics. In I. Noveck & D. Sperber (eds.). *Experimental Pragmatics*. 50—71. London: Palgrave.
Goffman, E. 1967. *Interaction Ritual: Essays in Face to Face Behavior*. New York: Garden City.
Golato, A. 2002. German compliment responses. *Journal of Pragmatics*, 34(5), 547—571.
Google Scholar 2018. Retrieved June 7, 2018 from https://en.wikipedia.org/wiki/Google_Scholar.
Gordon, C. 2013. 'You are killing your kids': Framing and impoliteness in a health makeover reality TV show. In N. Lorenzo-Dus & P. Blitvich (eds.). *Real Talk: Reality Television and Discourse Analysis in Action*. 245—265. New York: Palgrave Macmillan.
Graham, S. L. 2007. Disagreeing to agree: Conflict, (im)politeness and identity in a computer-mediated community. *Journal of Pragmatics*, 39(4), 742—759.
Graham, S. L. & Hardaker, C. 2017. (Im)politeness in digital communication. In J. Culpeper, M. Haugh, & D. Kádár. (eds.). *The Palgrave Handbook of Linguistic (im)politeness*. 785—814. London: Palgrave.
Grainger, K. 2011. 'First order' and 'second order' politeness: Institutional and intercultural

contexts. In Linguistic Politeness Research Group (ed.). *Discursive Approaches to Politeness*. 167—188. Berlin & New York: Mouton de Gruyter.

Green, G. M. 1996. *Pragmatics and Natural Language Understanding*. Hillsdale, N.J.: Erlbaum.

Grice, H. P. 1957. Meaning. *The Philosophical Review*, 66(3), 377—388.

Grice, H. P. 1969. Utterer's meaning and intention. *The Philosophical Review*, 78(2), 147—177.

Grice, H. P. 1975. Logic and conversation. In P. Cole & J. Morgan (eds.). *Syntax and Semantics 3: Speech Acts*. 41—58. London: Academic Press.

Grice, H. P. 1978. Further notes on logic and conversation. In P. Cole & J. Morgan. (eds.). *Syntax and Semantics 3: Speech Acts*. 113—128. London: Academic Press.

Grice, H. P. 1989. *Studies in the Way of Words*. Cambridge, MA: Harvard University Press.

Gu, Y. G. 1990. Politeness phenomena in modern Chinese. *Journal of Pragmatics*, 14(2), 237—257.

Gu, Y. G. 1993. The impasse of perlocution. *Journal of Pragmatics*, 20(5), 405—432.

Gu, Y. G. 1994. Pragmatics and rhetoric: a collaborative approach to conversation. In H. Parret. (ed.). *Pretending to Communicate*. 173—195. Berlin: Walter de Gruyter.

Halliday, M. A. K. & C. Matthiessen. 2014. *An Introduction to Functional Grammar* (4th Edition). London: Routledge.

Hardaker, C. 2010. Trolling in asynchronous computer-mediated communication: From user discussions to academic definitions. *Journal of Politeness Research*. 6, 215—242.

Harnish, R. M. 1976. Logical form and implicature. In T., Beaver, J., Katz & D. T. Langendoen. (eds.). *An Integrated Theory of Linguistic Ability*. 313—92. New York: Crowell.

Harnish, R. M. 1994. Mood, meaning and speech acts. In S. L. Tsohatzidis. (ed.). *Foundations of Speech Act Theory: Philosophical and Linguistic Perspectives*. 407—459. London: Routledge.

Harris, S. G. 1984. *Culture and Learning: Tradition and Education in North-East Arnhem Land*. Canberra: Australian Institute of Aboriginal Studies.

Harris, R. A. 1995. *The Linguistics Wars*. Oxford: Oxford University Press.

Haugh, M. 2007. The discursive challenge to politeness research: An interactional alternative. *Journal of Politeness Research*, 3(2), 295—317.

Haugh, M. 2018. Afterword: Theorizing (im)politeness. *Journal of Politeness Research* 14(1): 153—165.

Heim, I. 1983. On the Projection Problem for Presuppositions. In P. Portner & B. H. Partee (eds.), *Formal Semantics-the Essential Readings*. 249—260. Oxford: Blackwell.

Heim, I. 1992. Presupposition projection and the semantics of attitude verbs. *Journal of Semantics*, 9(3), 183—221.

Herrick, J. A. 2013. *History and Theory of Rhetoric: An Introduction*. (5th Edition). Upper Saddle River: Pearson.

Ho, Y. F. 1976. On the concept of face. *American Journal of Sociology*, 81(4), 867—884.

Holmes, J. 1988. Paying compliments: A sex-preferential politeness strategy. *Journal of Pragmatics*, 12(4), 445—465.

Holmes, J. 2005. Politeness and postmodernism — an appropriate approach to the analysis of language and gender?. *Journal of Sociolinguistics*, 9(1), 108—117.

Holmes, J. & Stubbe, M. 2014. *Power and Politeness in the Workplace: A Sociolinguistic Analysis of Talk at Work*. London & New York: Routledge.

Hong, G. 2005. *Research Methodology in Cross-cultural Pragmatics: An Inquiry into Data Collection Procedures*. Beijing: Foreign Language Teaching and Research Press.

Hong, W. 1996. An empirical study of Chinese request strategies. *International Journal of the Sociology of Language*, 122(1), 127—138.

Horn, L. R. 1984. Toward a new taxonomy for pragmatic inference: Q-based and R-based implicature. In D. Schiffrin. (ed.). *Meaning, Form, and Use in Context: Linguistic Applications*. 11—42. Washington DC: Georgetown University Press.

Horn, L. R. 1985. Metalinguistic negation and pragmatic ambiguity. *Language*, 61(1), 121—174.

Horn, L. R. 2012. Implying and inferring. In K. Allan & K. Jaszczolt. (eds.). *The Cambridge Handbook of Pragmatics*. 69—86. Cambridge: Cambridge University Press.

Horn, L. & Ward, G. (eds.). 2004. *The Handbook of Pragmatics*. Oxford: Blackwell.

Huang, E. 2017. Chinese people mean something very different when they send you a smiley emoji. Retrieved from https://qz.com/944693/chinese-people-mean-something-very-different-when-they-send-you-a-smiley-emoji/.

Huang, Y. 2007. *Pragmatics*. Oxford: Oxford University Press.

Huang, Y. 2013. Micro-and Macro-Pragmatics: Remapping Their Terrains. *International Review of Pragmatics*, 5(1), 129—162.

Huang, Y. 2014. *Pragmatics* (2nd Edition). Oxford: Oxford University Press.

Huang, Y. 2017. Introduction: What is Pragmatics. In Y. Huang (ed.). *The Oxford Handbook of Pragmatics*. 1—20. Oxford: Oxford University Press.

Huang, Y. 2018. Unarticulated constituents and neo-Gricean pragmatics. *Language and Linguistics*, 19(1), 1—31.

Ide, S. 1989. Formal forms and discernment: Two neglected aspects of universals of linguistic politeness. *Multilingua*, 8(2—3), 223—248.

Ishihara, N. 2010. Collecting data reflecting the pragmatic use of language. In B. Ishihara & A. D. Cohen. (eds.). *Teaching and Learning Pragmatics: Where Language and Culture Meet*. 37—55. Harlow: Longman.

Jaszczolt, K. 2005. *Default Semantics: Foundations of a Compositional Theory of Acts of Communication*. Oxford: Oxford University Press.

Jewitt, C. (ed.). 2009. *The Routledge Handbook of Multimodal Analysis*. London: Routledge.

Jia, M. & Xiang, M. Y. 2018. Neo-economy Principle in politeness: A case of Chinese online forum requests. Paper presented at the 11th International Conference on Im/politeness, Valencia, Spain.

Jiang, W. Q. 2000. *Pragmatics: Theory and Applications*. Beijing: Peking University Press.

Johns, A. & Félix-Brasdefer, J. C. 2015. Linguistic politeness and pragmatic variation in request production in Dakar French. *Journal of Politeness Research*, 11(1), 131—164.

Juanchich, M., Sirota, M., & Bonnefon, J. F. 2019. The polite wiggle-room effect in charity donation decisions. *Journal of Behavioral Decision Making*, 32(2), 179—193.

Kádár, D. Z. & Haugh, M. 2013. *Understanding Politeness*. Cambridge: Cambridge University Press.

Karttunen, L. 1973. Presuppositions of compound sentences. *Linguistic Inquiry*, 4(2), 169—193.

Karttunen, L. 1974. Presupposition and linguistic context. *Theoretical Linguistics*, 1(1), 181—194.

Kasanga, L. & Lwanga-Lumu, J. 2007. Cross-cultural linguistic realization of politeness: A study of apologies in English and Setswana. *Journal of Politeness Research*, 3(1), 65—92.

Kasper, G. 1990. Linguistic politeness: current research issues. *Journal of Pragmatics*, 14(2), 193—218.

Kasper, G. & Blum-Kulka, S. 1993. *Interlanguage Pragmatics*. New York: Oxford University Press.

Kasper, G. & Dahl, M. 1991. Research methods in interlanguage pragmatics. *Studies in Second Language Acquisition*, 13(2), 215—247.

Kavanagh, B. 2016. Emoticons as a medium for channeling politeness within American and Japanese online blogging communities. *Language & Communication*, 48, 53—65.

Keenan, E. O. 1976. The universality of conversational postulates. *Language in Society*, 5(1), 67—80.

Kim H. T. & Farashaiya, A. 2012. Utilizing formulaic request strategies in an ESL classroom. *Procedia-Social and Behavioral Sciences*, 59, 42—46.

Kripke, S. 1980. *Naming and Necessity*. Oxford: Blackwell.

Kuhn, T. S. 1962. *The Structure of Scientific Revolutions*. Chicago: University of Chicago Press.

Lachenicht, L. G. 1980. Aggravating language a study of abusive and insulting language. *Research on Language & Social Interaction*, 13(4), 607—687.

Lakoff, R. T. 1973. The logic of politeness; or, minding your Ps and Qs. *Chicago Linguistic Society*, 8, 292—305.

Leech, G. 1980. *Explorations in Semantics and Pragmatics*. Amsterdam: John Benjamins.

Leech, G. 1981. *Semantics: The Study of Meaning* (2nd Edition). Middlesex: Penguin Books.

Leech, G. 1983. *Principles of Pragmatics*. London & New York: Longman.

Leech, G. 1999. The distribution and function of vocatives in American and British English conversation. *Language and Computers*, 26(1), 107—120.

Leech, G. 2007. Politeness: Is there an East-West divide?. *Journal of Politeness Research*, 3(2), 167—206.

Leech, G. 2014. *The Pragmatics of Politeness*. Oxford: Oxford University Press.

Lee-Wong, S. M. 1994. Imperatives in requests: direct or impolite — observations from Chinese. *Pragmatics*, 4(4), 491—515.

Lee-Wong, S. M. 1998. Face support—Chinese particles as mitigators: A study of BA A/YA and NE. *Pragmatics*, 8(3), 387—404.

Levenston, E. A., & Blum, S. 1978. Discourse-completion as a technique for studying lexical features of interlanguage. *Working Papers in Bilingualism*, 15, 13—21.

Levinson, S. C. 1983. *Pragmatics*. Cambridge: Cambridge University Press.

Levinson, S. C. 1987. Pragmatics and the grammar of anaphora: a partial pragmatic reduction of binding and control phenomena. *Journal of Linguistics*, 23(2), 379—434.

Levinson, S. C. 1991. Pragmatic reduction of the binding conditions revisited. *Journal of Linguistics*, 27(1), 107—161.

Levinson, S. C. 2000. *Presumptive Meanings: The Theory of Generalized Conversational Implicature*. Cambridge, MA: MIT Press.

Li, C. N. & S. A., Thompson. 1976. Subject and Topic: A New Typology of Language. In C. N. Li (ed.). *Subject and Topic*. 466—471. London & New York: Academic Press.

Liu, R. Q. & Wen, X. 2006. *Linguistics: A New Coursebook*. Beijing: Foreign Language Teaching and Research Press.

Liu, Y. & Zhu, C. 2011. Rhetoric as the antistrophos of pragmatics: Toward a "competition of cooperation" in the study of language use. *Journal of Pragmatics*, 43(14), 3403—3415.

Locher, M. A. 2004. *Power and Politeness in Action: Disagreements in Oral Communication*. Berlin: Mouton de Gruyter.

Locher, M. A. 2006. Polite behavior within relational work: The discursive approach to politeness. *Multilingua*, 25(3), 249—267.

Locher, M. A. 2015. Interpersonal pragmatics and its link to (im)politeness research. *Journal of Pragmatics*, 86, 5—10.

Locher, M. A., & Graham, S. L. (eds.). 2010. *Interpersonal Pragmatics*. Berlin: Walter de Gruyter.

Locher, M. A., & Watts, R. J. 2005. Politeness theory and relational work. *Journal of Politeness Research*, 1(1), 9—33.

Lyons, J. 1977a. *Semantics* (Vol. 1). New York: Cambridge University Press,

Lyons, J. 1977b. *Semantics* (Vol. 2). New York: Cambridge University Press.

Lyons, J. 1995. *Linguistic Semantics: An Introduction*. Cambridge: Cambridge University Press.

MacFarlane, J. 2009. Nonindexical Contextualism. *Synthesis*, 166, 231—250.

Mao, L. R. 1994. Beyond politeness theory: 'Face' revisited and renewed. *Journal of Pragmatics*, 21(5), 451—486.

Marcu, D. 2000. Perlocutions: The Achilles' heel of speech act theory. *Journal of Pragmatics*, 32(12), 1719—1741.

Maricic, I. 2001. "Cyberpoliteness: Requesting strategies on *The Linguist List*." Paper presented at the *Seventh Conference of the International Pragmatics Association*, Budapest, Hungary.

Marti, L. 2006. Indirectness and politeness in Turkish-German bilingual and Turkish monolingual requests. *Journal of Pragmatics*, 38(11), 1836—1869.

Matsumoto, Y. 1989. Politeness and conversational universals-observations from Japanese. *Multilingua*, 8(2—3), 207—222.

Meier, A. J. 1995. Defining politeness: Universality in appropriateness. *Language Sciences*, 17(4), 345—356.

Merritt, M. 1976. On questions following questions in service encounters. *Language in Society*, 5(3), 315—357.

Mey J. L. 2001. *Pragmatics: An Introduction* (2nd Edition). UK: Blackwell.

Mills, S. 2003. *Gender and Politeness*. Cambridge: Cambridge University Press.

Mills, S. 2005. Gender and impoliteness. *Journal of Politeness Research*, 1(2), 263—280.

Mills, S. 2011. Discursive approaches to politeness and impoliteness. In Linguistic Politeness Research Group (ed.). *Discursive Approaches to Politeness*. 19—56. Berlin & New York: Mouton de Gruyter.

Morris, C. W. 1938. *Foundations of the Theory of Signs*. Chicago: University of Chicago Press.

Murphy, J. 2019. I'm sorry you are such an arsehole: (non-)canonical apologies and their implications for (im)politeness. *Journal of Pragmatics*, 142, 223—232.

Noveck, I. & Sperber, D. (eds.). 2005. *Experimental Pragmatics*. London: Palgrave.

Nunan, D. 1992. *Research Methods in Language Learning*. Cambridge: Cambridge University Press.

O'Driscoll, J. 2007. Brown & Levinson's face: How it can—and can't—help us to understand interaction across cultures. *Intercultural Pragmatics*, 4(4), 463—492.

Ogiermann, E. 2009a. *On Apologising in Negative and Positive Politeness Cultures*. Amsterdam: John Benjamins.

Ogiermann, E. 2009b. Politeness and in-directness across cultures: A comparison of English, German, Polish and Russian requests. *Journal of Politeness Research*, 5(2), 189—216.

Östman, J. O. 1995. Pragmatic particles twenty years after. In *Organization in discourse: Proceeding from the Turku Conference*. 95—108. Turku: University of Turku.

Pan, Y., & D. Kádár. 2011. Historical vs. contemporary Chinese linguistic politeness. *Journal of Pragmatics*, 43(6), 1525—1539.

Peccei, J. S. 1999. *Pragmatics*. London: Taylor & Francis.

Pinkham, J. 2000. *The Translator's Guide to Chinglish*. Beijing: Foreign Language Teaching and Research Press.

Pomerantz, A. 1975. Second Assessments: A Study of Some Features of Agreements/Disagreements. Unpublished PhD dissertation, University of California, Irvine.

Pomerantz, A. 1984. Agreeing and disagreeing with assessments: Some features of preferred/dispreferred turn shaped. In J. M. Atkinson & J. Heritage (eds.). *Structures of Social Action: Studies in Conversation Analysis*. 79—112. Cambridge: Cambridge University Press.

Poole, S. C. 1999. *An Introduction to Linguistics*. London: Macmillan Publishers.

Posner, R. 1987. Charles Morris and the behavioral foundations of semiotics. In M. Krampen, K. Oehler, R. Posner, & T. A. Sebeok (eds.). *Classics of Semiotics*. 23—57. New York: Plemun Press.

Potts, C. 2005. *The Logic of Conventional Implicatures*. Oxford: Oxford University Press.

Powell, M., Levy, D., Riley-Mukavetz, A., Brooks-Gillies, M., Novotny, M. & Fisch-Ferguson, J. 2014. Our story begins here: Constellating cultural rhetorics. *Enculturation*, 18. Retrieved from http://enculturation.net/our-story-begins-here.

Quaglio, P. 2009. *Television Dialogue: The Sitcom Friends vs. Natural Conversation*. Amsterdam/Philadelphia: John Benjamins.

Recanati, F. 1989. The pragmatics of what is said. *Mind & Language*, 4(4), 295—329.

Recanati, F. 2004. *Literal Meaning*. Cambridge: Cambridge University Press.

Rosaldo, M. Z. 1982. The things we do with words: Ilongot speech acts and speech act theory in philosophy. *Language in Society*, 11(2), 203—237.

Ross, J. R. 1970. On declarative sentences. In R. Jacobs & P. S. Rosenbaum. (eds.). *Readings in English Transformational Grammar*. 222—272. Waltham: Ginn.

Rühlemann & Aijmer, 2015. Corpus pragmatics: Laying the foundations. In K. Aijmer & C. Rühlemann, (eds.). *Corpus Pragmatics*. 1—26. Cambridge: Cambridge University Press.

Russell, B. 1905. On denoting. *Mind*, 14, 479—493.

Ruzickova, E. 2007. Strong and mild requestive hints and positive-face redress in Cuban Spanish. *Journal of Pragmatics*, 39(6), 1170—1202.

Sacks, H., Schegloff, E. A. & Jefferson, G. 1974. A simplest systematics for the organization of turn-taking for conversation. *Language*, 50(4), 696—735.

Sadock, J. M. 1974. *Toward a Linguistic Theory of Speech Acts*. New York: Academic Press.

Sadock, J. M. 1994. Toward a Grammatically Realistic Typology of Speech Acts. In S. L. Tsohatzidis. (ed.). *Foundations of Speech Act Theory: Philosophical and Linguistic Perspectives*. 393—406. London: Routledge.

Sadock, J. M. 2006. Speech acts. In L. R. Horn & G. Ward. (eds.). *The Handbook of Pragmatics*. 53—73. Oxford: Blackwell.

Saeed, J. I. 2009. *Semantics* (3rd Edition). Oxford: Blackwell.

Saul, J. M. 2002. What is said and psychological reality: Grice's project and relevance

theorists' criticisms. *Linguistics and Philosophy*, 25(3), 347—372.
Schegloff, E. A. 1968. Sequencing in conversational openings. *American Anthropologist*, 70(6), 1075—1095.
Schegloff, E. A. & Sacks, H. 1973. Opening up closings. *Semiotica*, 8(4), 289—327.
Scollon, R. & Scollon, S. W. 1995. *Intercultural Communication: A Discourse Approach*. Oxford: Blackwell.
Searle, J. R. 1969. *Speech Acts: An Essay in the Philosophy of Language*. Cambridge: Cambridge University Press.
Searle, J. R. 1975. Indirect speech acts. In P. Cole & J. Morgan (eds.). *Syntax and Semantics 3: Speech Acts*. 59—82. London: Academic Press.
Searle, J. R. 1979. *Expression and Meaning: Studies in the Theory of Speech Acts*. Cambridge: Cambridge University Press.
Shibamoto-Smith, J. S. 2011. Honorifics, "politeness," and power in Japanese political debate. *Journal of Pragmatics*, 43(15), 3707—3719.
Sifianou, M. 1997. Politeness and off-record indirectness. *International Journal of the Sociology of Language*, 126(1), 163—180.
Spencer-Oatey, H. 2002. Managing rapport in talk: Using rapport sensitive incidents to explore the motivational concerns underlying the management of relations. *Journal of Pragmatics*, 34(5), 529—545.
Spencer-Oatey, H., Ng, P. & Dong, L. 2008. British and Chinese reactions to compliment responses. In H. Spencer-Oatey (ed.). *Culturally Speaking: Managing Rapport Through Talk Across Cultures* (2nd Edition), 95—117. London: Continuum.
Sperber, D. & Wilson, D. 1995. *Relevance: Communication and Cognition* (2nd Edition). Oxford: Blackwell.
Stalnaker, R. C. 1973. Presuppositions. *Journal of Philosophical Logic*, 2, 447—457.
Stanley, J. 2007. *Language in Context: Selected Essays*. Oxford: Oxford University Press.
Stasko, J., Gorg, C., Liu, Z. & Singhal, K. 2008. Jigsaw: supporting investigative analysis through interactive visualization. *Information Visualization*, 7(2), 118—132.
Stokoe, E. 2008. Dispreferred actions and other interactional breaches as devices for occasioning audience laughter in television "sitcoms". *Social Semiotics*, 18(3), 289—307.
Strawson, P. F. 1950. On referring. *Mind*, 59, 320—344.
Strawson, P. F. 1964. Intention and convention in speech acts. *Philosophical Review*, 73(4), 439—460.
Strawson, P. F. 1971. Intention and convention in speech acts. In Searle J. R. (ed.). *The Philosophy of Language*. 23—38. London: Oxford University Press.
Streeck, J. 2009. *Gesturecraft: The Manu-facturing of Meaning* Amsterdam: John Benjamins.
Struck, W. & E. B. White. 1999. *The Elements of Style* (4th Edition). New York: Longman.
Swales, J. 1990. *Genre analysis: English in academic and research settings*. Cambridge: Cambridge University Press.
Talmy, L. 1988. Force dynamics in language and cognition. *Cognitive Science*, 12(1), 49—100.
Taylor, T. J., & Cameron, D. 1987. *Analyzing Conversation: Rules and Units in the Structure of Talk*. New York: Pergamon.
Terasaki, A. K. 2004. Pre-announcement sequences in conversation. In G. H. Lerner (ed.). *Conversation Analysis: Studies from the First Generation*. 171 — 224. Amsterdam & Philadelphia: John Benjamins.

Terkourafi, M. 2001. *Politeness in Cypriot Greek: A Frame-based Approach*. Unpublished doctoral dissertation, University of Cambridge.

Terkourafi, M. 2005. Beyond the micro-level in politeness research. *Journal of Politeness Research*, 1(1), 237—262.

Terkourafi, M. 2008. Toward a unified theory of politeness, impoliteness, and rudeness. In D. Bousfield & M. A. Locher (eds.). *Impoliteness in Language: Studies on Its Interplay with Power in Theory and Practice*. 45—74. Berlin & New York: Mouton de Gruyter.

Terkourafi, M. 2015. Conventionalization: A new agenda for im/politeness research. *Journal of Pragmatics*, 86, 11—18.

Thomas, J. 1995. *Meaning in Interaction: An Introduction to Pragmatics*. London: Longman.

Travis, C. 2008. *Occasion-Sensitivity: Selected Essays*. Oxford: Oxford University Press.

Trudgill, P. 2000. *Sociolinguistics: An Introduction to Language and Society*. (4th Edition). London: Penguin.

van der Bom I & Mills, S. 2015. A discursive approach to the analysis of politeness data. *Journal of Politeness Research*, 11(2), 179—206.

Verschueren, J. 1999. *Understanding pragmatics*. New York: Oxford University Press.

Watts, R. J. 1992. Linguistic politeness and politic verbal behavior: Reconsidering claims for universality. In R. J. Watts, S. Ide & K. Ehlich (eds.). *Politeness in Language: Studies in Its History, Theory and Practice*. 43—69. Berlin & New York: Mouton de Gruyter.

Watts, R. J. 2003. *Politeness*. Cambridge: Cambridge University Press.

Wedding Reception Venues near Newry, ME. n. d. Retrieved June 1, 2018, from https://www.theknot.com/marketplace/wedding-reception-venues-newry-me.

Wierzbicka, A. 1987. *English Speech Act Verbs: A Semantic Dictionary*. Sydney: Academic Press.

Wilson, D. 1975. *Presuppositions and Non-Truth Conditional Semantics*. New York: Academic Press.

Wilson, D. & Sperber, D. 1991. Inference and implicature. In S. Davis (ed.). *Pragmatics: A Reader*. 377—393. New York: Oxford University Press.

World Population. 2018. Retrieved May 31, 2018, from http://worldpopulationreview.com/continents/world-population/.

Wray, A., Trott, K., Broomer, A., Reay, S. & Butler, C. 1998. *Projects in Linguistics: A Practical Guide to Researching Language*. London: Arnold.

Xiang, M. Y. 2017. Toward a Neo-economy Principle in pragmatics. *Journal of Pragmatics*, 107, 31—45.

Yule, G. 1996. *Pragmatics*. Oxford: Oxford University Press.

Yus, F. 2011. *Cyberpragmatics: Internet-mediated Communication in Context*. Amsterdam: John Benjamins.

Zhu, H., Li, W. & Qian, Y. 2000. The sequential organisation of gift offering and acceptance in Chinese. *Journal of Pragmatics*, 32(1), 81—103.

Zipf, G. K. 1949. *Human Behaviour and the Principle of Least Effort*. Cambridge, MA: Addison-Wesley.

曹笃鑫、向明友,2017. 意义研究的流变:语义—语用界面视角,《外语与外语教学》第 4 期,78—89 页。

陈新仁,2015. 语义学与语用学的分界:一种新方案,《外语教学与研究》第 6 期,838—849 页。

杜世洪,2005。《美国语言之旅》。北京:中国社会科学出版社。

黄高才,2016。《中国文化概论(第二版)》。北京:北京大学出版社。

李杰、陈超美,2017。《CiteSpace:科技文本挖掘及可视化(第二版)》。北京:首都经济贸易大学出版社。

刘风光、邓耀臣、肇迎如,2016。中美政治道歉言语行为对比研究,《外语与外语教学》第6期,42—55页。

刘丽娟,2010。面子理论视野中的网络聊天礼貌策略研究,《河南社会科学》第3期,120—122页。

刘敏,2014。中英文学术搜索引擎的对比研究,《图书馆学研究》第24期,29—35页。

刘绍忠,2000。"请"字用法汉英对比与语用负迁移,《外国语(上海外国语大学学报)》第5期,9—16页。

刘蜀、于国栋,2018。汉语言语交际中前序列与前序序列的会话分析研究——以请求行为为例,《外语教学》第2期,30—35页。

穆军芳、马美茹,2016。国际批评话语分析研究进展的科学知识图谱分析(2006—2015年),《河北大学学报(哲学社会科学版)》第6期,146—154页。

冉永平,2018。我国的人际语用学前沿研究,《外语教学》第3期,37—39页。

冉永平、刘平,2015。人际语用学视角下的关系研究,《外语教学》第4期,1—7页。

孙三军、周晓岩,2011。《语言研究:方法与工具》。合肥:安徽大学出版社。

孙毅,2015。当代隐喻学在中国(1994—2013)——一项基于CSSCI外国语言学来源期刊的文献计量研究,《西安外国语大学学报》第3期,17—22页。

汪奎,2012。网络会话中"呵呵"的功能研究。硕士学位论文,华东师范大学。

杨国萍、向明友,2018。国外语法化研究趋势探究:来自知识图谱的动态计量,《外语教学》第1期,26—31页,76页。

于国栋,2008。《会话分析》。上海:上海外语教育出版社。

袁周敏、刘环环,2017。国际中介语语用学研究动态可视化分析,《外语教学与研究》第3期,456—463页。

夏登山、殷彩艳、蓝纯,2017。三方恭维回应策略研究,《外语教学与研究》第5期,688—698页。

向明友,1995。现代汉语呼语之管见,《西南大学学报(社会科学版)》第3期,117—120页。

向明友,2008。语用三律,《外语教学》第2期,1—5页。

向明友,2015。语用学研究的知识图谱分析。《外国语》第6期,36—47页。

向明友,2018。言语行为理论评注,《现代外语》第4期,541—549页。

谢智敏、郭倩玲,2017。基于深度学习的学术搜索引擎——Semantic Scholar,《情报杂志》第8期,175—182页。

薛冰、向明友,2018。近十年国际语料库隐喻研究的知识图谱分析,《解放军外国语学院学报》第4期,43—51页。

翟中会,2015。Google与Google学术及图书馆传统数据库差异性研究,《图书馆工作与研究》第12期,31—33页。

赵蓉英、陈烨,2014。学术搜索引擎Google Scholar和Microsoft Academic Search的比较研

究,《情报科学》第 2 期,3—6 页。
赵燚、向明友,2018。关联理论研究前沿探析,《现代外语》第 1 期,130—140 页。
朱永生,2007。多模态话语分析的理论基础与研究方法,《外语学刊》第 5 期,82—86 页。

Appendix One Resources

To help beginners engage in a deeper study of pragmatics, below is a brief sketch of textbooks, handbooks, collections, dictionaries, journals, and conference papers of pragmatics published and circulated internationally:

Textbooks

Chen, X. R. 2009. *A New Coursebook in Pragmatics*. Beijing: Foreign Language Teaching and Research Press.
Cummings, L. 2005. *Pragmatics: A Multidisciplinary Perspective*. Edinburgh: Edinburgh University Press.
Green, G. M. 2012. *Pragmatics and Natural Language Understanding*. London: Routledge.
Huang, Y. 2014. *Pragmatics* (2nd Edition). Oxford: Oxford University Press.
Jiang, W. Q. 2000. *Pragmatics: Theory and Applications*. Beijing: Beijing University Press.
Leech, G. 1983. *Principles of Pragmatics*. London & New York: Longman.
Levinson, S. C. 1983. *Pragmatics*. Cambridge: Cambridge University Press.
Mey J. L. 2001. *Pragmatics: An Introduction* (2nd Edition). UK: Blackwell.
Peccei, J. S. 1999. *Pragmatics*. London: Taylor & Francis.
Poole, S. C. 1999. *An Introduction to Linguistics*. London: Macmillan Publishers.
Thomas, J. 1995. *Meaning in Interaction: An Introduction to Pragmatics*. London: Longman.
Verschueren, J. 1999. *Understanding Pragmatics*. London: Routledge.
Yule, G. 1996. *Pragmatics*. Oxford: Oxford University Press.
何自然、冉永平,2009。《新编语用学概论》。北京:北京大学出版社。
钱冠连,1997。《汉语文化语用学》。北京:清华大学出版社。

Handbooks

Allan, K. & K. M. Jaszczolt (eds.). 2012. *The Cambridge Handbook of Pragmatics*. Cambridge: Cambridge University Press.
Barron, A., Y. G., Gu & G. Steen. (eds.). 2017. *The Routledge Handbook of Pragmatics*. London: Routledge.
Horn, L. & G. Ward. (eds.). 2004. *The Handbook of Pragmatics*. Oxford: Blackwell.
Huang, Y. (ed.). 2017. *The Oxford Handbook of Pragmatics*. Oxford: Oxford University Press.
Verschueren, J., Östman, J., Blommaert, J. O. & C. Bulcaen. (eds.). 1995. *Handbook of Pragmatics*. Amsterdam: John Benjamins. This handbook series is published annually since 1995.

Collections in specific areas

Aijmer, K. & Rühlemann, C. (eds.). 2015. *Corpus Pragmatics*. Cambridge: Cambridge University Press.
Culpeper, J., Haugh, M., & Kádár, D. Z. (eds.). 2017. *The Palgrave Handbook of Linguistic (Im)politeness*. London: Palgrave Macmillan.
Herring, S., Stein, D. & Virtanen, T. (eds.). (2013). *Pragmatics of Computer-Mediated*

    Communication. Berlin: Walter de Gruyter.
Jucker, A. H., Schneider, K. P. & Wolfram, B. (eds.). (2018). *Methods in Pragmatics*. Berlin & Boston: De Gruyter Mouton.
Kasper, G. & Blum-Kulka, S. (eds.). 1993. *Interlanguage Pragmatics*. Oxford: Oxford University Press.
Linguistic Politeness Research Group (ed.). 2011. *Discursive Approaches to Politeness*. Berlin: Walter de Gruyter.
Locher, M. A. & Graham, S. L. (eds.). 2010. *Interpersonal Pragmatics*. Berlin: Walter de Gruyter.
Noveck, I. & Sperber, D. (eds.). 2005. *Experimental Pragmatics*. London: Palgrave.
Taguchi, N. (2019). *The Routledge Handbook of Second Language Acquisition and Pragmatics*. New York, NY: Routledge.
Tipton, R. & Desilla, L. (2019) *The Routledge Handbook of Translation and Pragmatics*. New York, NY: Routledge.
Zienkowski, J., Östman, J. O. & Verschueren, J. (eds.). 2011. *Discursive Pragmatics*. Amsterdam & New York: John Benjamins Publishing.

Dictionaries

Allott, N. 2010. *Key Terms in Pragmatics*. New York: Bloomsbury Publishing.
Cruse, A. 2006. *Glossary of Semantics and Pragmatics*. Edinburgh: Edinburgh University Press.
Huang, Y. 2012. *The Oxford Dictionary of Pragmatics*. Oxford: Oxford University Press.

Journals (2021—10—30)

Argumentation
    https://link.springer.com/journal/10503
Corpus Pragmatics
    https://link.springer.com/journal/41701
Discourse Processes
    https://www.tandfonline.com/toc/hdsp20/current
Language & Communication
    https://www.journals.elsevier.com/language-and-communication/
Language Sciences
    https://www.journals.elsevier.com/language-sciences/
Lingua
    https://www.journals.elsevier.com/lingua/
Linguistics
    https://www.degruyter.com/view/j/ling
Intercultural Pragmatics
    https://www.degruyter.com/view/j/iprg
International Journal of Language Communication Disorders
    https://onlinelibrary.wiley.com/journal/14606984
International Review of Pragmatics
    http://www.brill.com/international-review-pragmatics
Internet Pragmatics
    https://www.benjamins.com/#catalog/journals/ip/main

Journal of East Asian Pragmatics
    https://journals.equinoxpub.com/index.php/EAP
Journal of Historical Pragmatics
    https://benjamins.com/#catalog/journals/jhp
Journal of Language and Social Psychology
    https://journals.sagepub.com/home/jls
Journal of Language Aggression and Conflict
    https://benjamins.com/catalog/jlac
Journal of Politeness Research
    https://www.degruyter.com/view/j/jplr
Journal of Pragmatics
    https://www.journals.elsevier.com/journal-of-pragmatics/
Multilingua
    https://www.degruyter.com/view/j/mult
Pragmatics
    https://ipra.uantwerpen.be/main.aspx?c=*HOME&n=1360
Pragmatics & Cognition
    https://benjamins.com/#catalog/journals/pc/main
Pragmatics and Society
    http://www.jbe-platform.com/content/journals/18789722
Semantics and Pragmatics
    http://semprag.org
Text & Talk
    https://www.degruyter.com/view/j/text?lang=en

Conferences
全国语用学研讨会
Annual Conference of the Society for Text and Discourse
International Pragmatics Conference
International Conference of the American Pragmatics Association
International Conference on Intercultural Pragmatics and Communication
International Communication Association Annual Convention
International Conference on Language and Social Psychology
National Communication Association Annual Convention

Appendix Two　Research Notes

  While our efforts end here, there are still a lot more that remain undone in pragmatics. We leave the blanks below for you to note the works and phenomena you may observe, read, and encounter in your quest for pragmatics. We believe that these summaries will help you develop a clearer map of different research topics and grow your own research trajectories.

Topic: _____

Argument 1:

_____
_____
_____

Examples:

_____
_____
_____

Counterexamples:

_____
_____
_____

Argument 2:

_____
_____
_____

Examples:

_____
_____
_____

Counterexamples:

_____
_____
_____

Appendix Two Research Notes

Argument 3:
_____
_____
_____

Examples:
_____
_____
_____

Counterexamples:
_____
_____
_____

Method 1:
_____
_____
_____

Method 2:
_____
_____
_____

Method 3:
_____
_____
_____

Remaining Problems:
_____
_____
_____

Supported by "the Fundamental Research Funds for the Central Universities" in UIBE